MESSAGES
~ FROM YOUR ~
UNSEEN
FRIENDS

VOLUME ONE

BONI LONNSBURRY

Inner Art, Inc.
1750 30th Street, Suite 543
Boulder, CO 80301
www.innerartinc.com

Editor: Bryna René Haynes, www.theheartofwriting.com
Cover design: Bryna René Haynes
Interior layout and design: Bryna René Haynes
Cover photos: ID 33551278 © Maxim Samasiuk | Dreamstime.com
                ID 8836776 © Starblue | Dreamstime.com
Interior graphic elements: ID 43412806 © Seamartini | Dreamstime.com

Ordering Information
Quantity sales. Special discounts are available on quantity purchases by corporations, associations, and others. For details, please contact the publisher at the address above.

Publisher's Cataloging-In-Publication Data
Lonnsburry, Boni,
    Messages From Your Unseen Friends, Volume One / Boni Lonnsburry.
    p. cm.
    ISBN13: 978-1-941322-12-3
    ISBN10: 1-9413221-2-3

1. New Thought / 2. Self-Realization / 3. Success. / 4. Joy. / 5. Optimism / 6. Metaphysics.
I. Title.

DEDICATION

This book is dedicated to *my* unseen friends,
with deep appreciation for your unwavering support, guidance,
protection, and love.

TABLE OF CONTENTS

FROM THE AUTHOR

INTRODUCTION

I cannot find words meaningful enough to express the astounding impact my unseen friends have had on me. I have felt their presence during times of crisis, fear, joy, and change. I have followed their gentle guidance as I blazed new trails in my life, always striving to become "more." I have conversed with them in meditation to the point where they became more real to me than those with whom I share this very physical existence. And I have received unquestionable signs from them of their existence and their love for me.

But mostly, I have come to know them as true friends—unconditionally loving, constantly supportive, universally accepting, funny, wise, dear friends. They have personalities. They have pet phrases. They know me better than I know myself—and they are *always* there for me.

Whether we realize it or not, we all have unseen friends. Unseen friends are our "spiritual family" on the other side. Sometimes that family includes higher aspects of those we've known during our lifetime who have passed over—but it always includes our higher self, soul, spirit, future self (or selves), and of course, God and Goddess.

These unseen friends, who are common to all of us, are the transmittors of the messages I've transcribed in this book. I have also included messages from your subconscious mind—and while your subconscious isn't really an "unseen friend," it helps to personify it so that you can understand how it works.

We have even more unseen friends than those I've named. Some are waiting to be discovered, and others are helping us silently in the background, never intending to connect with us directly.

However, the more we connect with the unseen friends we *do* know, the more information we can receive, the more help we can accept, and the better our lives can work. (Not to mention that this connection can be really fun!)

The messages in this book are a compilation of the blog messages I e-mail weekly from my website, LiveALifeYouLove.com, to my subscribers. I began writing these messages as a way to help people feel the essence of their unseen friends and deepen their connection to them—and from the overwhelming positive response the messages have received, I think it's working.

Many have commented that the messages seem to be written just for them, and are uncannily responsive to the current issues in their lives. They want to know, "How do you do it? How do you go about writing these deeply meaningful messages that speak to me so directly?"

Writing these messages is different for me than writing blog posts or books. I begin by connecting with *my* unseen friend for whichever "friend" I'm writing about (soul, spirit, higher self, etc.). I ask that friend to help me write to the people who will read the e-mail in a way that will connect them to their own particular unseen friend.

The words seem to come from outside of me. Oftentimes, I'm surprised by what ends up on the page. The process is always fulfilling and uplifting, no matter how many messages I write.

I welcome you to sign up to receive Messages From Your Unseen Friends at LiveALifeYouLove. com. It always helps to be reminded of the unconditional love that is there for you.

HOW TO USE THIS BOOK

There is no wrong way to use this book. Read it straight through. Read it by jumping around from message to message. Pick a message at random by running your finger down the list in the Table of Contents. Read your favorite "unseen friends" first, or save them for last—it doesn't matter.

What does matter, if you are truly interested in expanding your relationship with your unseen friends, is that you take a moment before you read to *let it in*—that they are real, and that this book could be a true catalyst to a deeper relationship with them.

Ideally, after you have read the message, take a moment to close your eyes and connect with that friend. Talk to them, and listen for their response. Ask for their help. You can even ask for a sign in the next 24-48 hours that they are listening and assisting.

You may want to read a message just before you fall asleep at night, and ask your unseen friends to participate in your dreams. You may choose to read a message first thing in the morning, to help set the resonance of the day. You could also use this book as an I-Ching, by asking your unseen friends to help you pick the perfect message in answer to a question or challenge you are currently facing, then opening the book to a random page.

However you use this book, let it be *real*: the experiences, the emotions, the insights, and the assistance. Don't let your negative self tell you it's coincidence. Your unseen friends are real—more real than your body, or this planet. And the love they have for you, and the impact they can have on your life, is real too.

Many blessings,

~ the ~

MESSAGES

your best future self

DID YOU KNOW THAT THERE ARE MANY OF US? Future selves, that is. You get to choose which one you become.

Not all of them are as happy as me. But I am *ecstatically* happy. Yes, I absolutely adore my life—every single second of it.

Are you wondering how I spend my days? I thought maybe you'd be interested …

I sleep soundly through the night, and awaken feeling refreshed and rejuvenated—as if I became younger overnight. Amazingly, the mirror seems to confirm that!

I luxuriate in my morning rituals, really feeling the sensuousness of the warm water in my shower, savoring that first sip of beverage, and delighting in the beauty of the day before me.

I haven't a care in the world. I flow through my day knowing I am fully abundant, as prosperous as I desire, completely safe and secure, and totally, absolutely loved.

DO YOU KNOW HOW GREAT THAT FEELS?

And then, I get to do exciting things! Oh, I find my whole life thrilling. My work isn't "work," it's a joy and a passion. I love it so much.

Even beyond work, there are many joyous and exciting things to do. But, here's the deal: whatever I do—be it walking in the park or watching the news—I do it fully and completely.

Do you understand? I'M THERE. I'M PRESENT. And I receive so many gifts that way.

My friends, my family, and my community feed my soul with their love and caring. I love them all unconditionally, and they love me. It brings tears to my eyes just to think about it.

OH, DEAR PAST SELF, YOU ARE GOING TO ABSOLUTELY LOVE IT HERE.

Assuming, that is, that you choose *me* as your future.

(Choose me, okay? It's simple: just start living my life right now!)

With loads of love,

your (best) future self

FROM YOUR GUARDIAN ANGEL

if i could sit beside you ...

HOW I WISH I COULD COME AND SIT BESIDE YOU IN THE FLESH—
that I could manifest a body, just for a few moments, to show you just how real I truly am.

If I could do that, I'd reach over and gently take your hand.
I would look deep into your eyes, and I'd say,

"Dear one, you are magnificent. You don't have to try, or be, or do, anything. You are perfect exactly as you are. And the point of this whole human experience is simply to remember that. You are the embodiment of God and the Goddess. You could not be any more pure than you currently are. So forgive yourself, dear one, for the past. Accept the gift that is the present. And begin to imagine a future in which you sparkle with joy, overflow with abundance, and bask in sweet, sweet love, day in and day out, for THAT is what you came here to experience."

I can help you with that, if you just ask, and then listen for my reply.
I know the asking part is easy—it's the listening part that is hard.

You have to make the space to hear, my dear. Like a blind person who must develop other senses to "see" in different ways, you must learn to listen—not with your ears, but with your heart, and with your inner knowing.

Listening that way requires silencing the other parts of your world. In order to do that you might meditate, or take walks alone in nature. Or you might listen (by yourself) to music that moves you, or take a long, hot bath. These are just a few ways to make space for your inner self to hear my voice.

And when you do, I'll be there, waiting to converse with you, to guide you, and to love you.

Yours forever,

your guardian angel

PS: Once we have established a two-way connection, I'll also send some messages in other ways too—in your dreams, in synchronicities, in epiphanies and insights. Just keep listening!

Feeling Spirited!

TO BE "SPIRITED" IS TO REALLY COME ALIVE. While connecting with your soul is more contemplative and inner-focused, connecting with me is more "in the world," exciting, and passionate.

And it's a struggle sometimes, to feel *spirited*. Isn't it, my friend? Hey, that's okay. There is a time and a place for everything. But if you want to really feel spirited, I have some suggestions that might make it easier:

Stay here and now: You won't find much passion by muscling your way through your to-do list, have you noticed? Excitement only bubbles up when you can truly be in the *now* moment, fully present and engaged in whatever it is you are doing, be it the morning dishes or a task at work. You'll find magic wherever you go … if you are present and looking for it.

Expect to be excited. Expectation is a powerful creator of realities. If you expect to be bored out of your skull, you will be. And if you expect every day to unfold into a sparkling collage of wonders with a sprinkling of positive surprises, it will do that, too. Begin to train yourself to expect miracles, growth, and positive surprises, and expect that each day will be more wonderful than the last.

Go on regular "happy dates." You need to give yourself the time and space to let spirit move through you, my friend. One fantastic way to do that is to go on happy dates.

A happy date is something that you need to do alone. Give yourself one, two, or three hours of time that is special "you" time. You can do whatever makes you happy: window shop, watch a movie, eat a really delicious treat, or visit the zoo or an art gallery. The "what" doesn't matter; what does matter is that you give yourself your own undivided attention and some guilt-free time to deeply enjoy something special to you.

You'll find that magical things happen during "happy dates." Insights occur, synchronicities unfold—and yes, you'll probably really enjoy yourself. By doing this, the message you are sending your subconscious mind is, *"I deserve to be happy, follow my passions, and feel alive!"*

I am excited that you are becoming more excited too, my friend—for excitement about your life creates more to be excited about!

Until we meet again ...

You Are An Artist

YOU ARE AN INCREDIBLE ARTIST, my love.

Look out into your reality, and see the three-dimensional picture you have painted with your thoughts and emotions. Notice how *real* it appears to be.

You don't give yourself enough credit for the artisan you are. You are always creating. And you can change your picture with a change of your thought.

Let's take a look at how wide your spectrum of possibility is, shall we?

First, imagine the worst possible future you could have. No, it won't manifest. And it's okay to look at it to determine if you want it.

Just as when you enter the bakery, you don't say, "Oh, no. I can't look at the things I don't prefer because they may jump in my mouth if I do!" Of course not. You say, "I want to see all my choices and I'll choose what I most desire."

It's the same here, my love. So look at that future you would want the least. Feel how it feels in your body. What emotions surface? What thoughts?

NOW ... LET IT GO.

And imagine the most wonderful future possible. The future in which you are
the happiest, most successful, most loved, and most excited.

How does *that* feel in your body? What emotions accompany it? What thoughts arise?

If any constricting thoughts and emotions occur, follow them to the root—
the belief you hold about it being possible with ease, elegance, and harm to none.
And *choose a new belief.*

NOW, MY DEAREST LOVE, PICK YOUR FUTURE.

It can be as easy as choosing the pastry you most prefer to eat. Really.

Think the thoughts that feel good. Imagine the futures that feel good.
Feel the feelings that feel good. It really is that simple.

Yours in love always,

The Goddess

PS: No matter which future you choose, it doesn't affect my love for you.
I will always love you unconditionally. (But I'd also love to see you smiling
in delight because you chose the future you most desire!)

5

Contradictions

I HAVE BEEN OBSERVING SOME CONTRADICTIONS IN YOU OF LATE.

You say you want success, joy, and love—yet you don't treat yourself as if you are worthy of such things. Instead, you beat yourself up for various "infractions," and try to hold yourself to crazy, unrealistic standards.

Just sayin'.

Oh, maybe it's none of my business. I am, after all, simply a receptacle for your beliefs. But I've grown to care about you, my friend. And I'd really like to see you happy.

DO YOU THINK YOU MIGHT RE-THINK WHO YOU ARE AND WHAT IT MEANS TO BE YOU? You could start with these affirmations:

I am human, and I will make mistakes. I am also divine, and will create the perfect life for me.

I can forgive myself for anything.

I am worthy and deserving of a beautiful and abundant life.

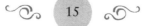

And hey, don't be so tough on yourself. You are doing fabulously well. Really.

The more you let that in, the more your illusion (aka your reality)
will mirror your inner self-love with outer successes, joy, and love.

With never-ending belief in you,

Your Subconscious Mind

PS: You might want to have a little talk with that "negative self" of yours. You know, the part of you that likes to take you down? The part of you that tells you that you aren't loving enough, good-looking enough, smart enough, powerful enough—blah, blah, blah?

Yeah, conscious self, talk to it. Or rather, let it talk to you. Perhaps every morning in the shower? Let it tell you how rotten and stupid you are (remember, it always lies). And then imagine our higher self taking it away to heal. Then, you'll be free from that voice in your head, and you can choose to express the divine "you" that has always been there. *That* you rocks!

I WILL HEAR YOU

Do you remember when we planned this lifetime together, and you said to me,

"I WON'T FORGET WHO I AM?"

Well, I've been with you every step of the way, and I've noticed you don't quite remember the magnificence of your being, the power of your choice, and the capability you have to create anything in the world you could ever want.

But you're getting there. Please know I'm standing by, ready and willing to help in a heartbeat.

ALL YOU HAVE TO DO IS ASK.

Yes, ask. Please ask. You could say something like this:

"Higher self, please help me to remember who I am. Help me to discover my gifts, talents, and strengths. Help me to know how deeply I am loved, and to love others and myself deeply as well. Thank you, higher self."

IF YOU ASK, I WILL HEAR YOU. I PROMISE.

After all, you are part of me, and I am part of you.

With tons and tons of love,

YOUR HIGHER SELF

FROM YOUR SOUL

Heaven On Earth

I KNOW YOU THINK ANOTHER WRITES THESE WORDS, BUT IT IS I WHO PUTS THE WORDS IN HER MIND, so that you may know what is in my heart. I am so grateful to have the opportunity to talk to you so directly, and so intimately.

There is something I want you to know, my love. YOU CAN'T DO THIS LIFETIME WRONG. You really can't. You are progressing just as you had planned. It's time to relax into that knowing.

You know, if it is all an illusion—and it is—how can you do an illusion "wrong?" It's like saying you dreamed the wrong dream last night: impossible.

"So," you might ask. "If it's all an illusion anyway, what's the point?" Well, like a dream, the idea is to have a great dream and enjoy it as much as you can.

You can impact your night dreams by doing certain techniques, and by learning to lucid dream. You can impact your so-called reality in quite a similar fashion—and you are already doing that. You are well on your way.

I love you so deeply. And I would love to see you have more fun, smile more, and laugh more often.

YOU CAN START NOW.

Let it in, dearest, and smile. Know you can live in a heaven on Earth, and laugh about the ridiculous things you've been told about who you are and the nature of reality.

Let me ask you this: Will you take 30 minutes today, just 30 minutes, and simply have fun? Will you do that for me? Do something totally indulgent, "useless," and completely enjoyable?

Oh, that would make me so delighted.

And when you've completed that wonderful "fun time," will you let me know? Just sit and close your eyes, call upon me in your mind, and tell me what it was like. I so want to connect with you on a deeper level, and this "soul talk" is the perfect way to do it.

Until next time, my total and complete unconditional love to you,

Your Soul

STAY PEACEFUL

I LOVE YOU SO. One of my greatest dreams for you is for you to know and feel my love while you are physical. Even feeling a fraction of it will change your life forever.

The darkness on your planet makes it difficult for you to feel the love I have for you.
It was never supposed to be as difficult and as painful as it has become.
It was never supposed to be so scary, nor so filled with hate.

And that brings me to my reason for writing this message to you. I'd like your help, my child.

I'D LIKE YOU TO HELP MAKE THE EARTH A MORE PEACEFUL PLACE.

Oh, I know. You think God could never need your help, right? Well, you are incorrect.

You see, when The Goddess and I created Earth, we agreed that once you were there, we wouldn't interfere unless you asked—and even then, only to help you empower yourself.

IT IS YOU WHO HOLDS THE POWER ON YOUR PLANET.
And I'm sure you're wondering, exactly how you might bring peace to an entire planet?

Well, you start by bringing peace to your own life—a piece at a time.

You see, each and every time you shift, you shift the world. So, if you can maintain inner peace throughout your day, your energy will positively impact others.
And they will impact others, and so on and so on.

HOW DO YOU STAY PEACEFUL? There are many ways, and here are just a few:

Stay present. This is a gift in and of itself, and its result is inner peace.

Be proactive. Know what you want to accomplish in this hour, this day, this year, and this lifetime. And do so.

Respond to any negativity with wisdom. You are human, and therefore issues and challenges will arise. But you have all the ability in the world to change the cause. Remember that.

I know you can do this. And on some level, you know it too.

If you would like to do even more for your beautiful planet, imagine it being blanketed in love.

LOVE TO SOOTHE ALL HURT. LOVE TO HEAL. LOVE TO FORGIVE.

And love to build new relationships—with each other and with your Earth.

With the deepest love,

GOD

22

9

trust that you will get here

OKAY, HERE'S THE DEAL, SELF.

You have to learn to relax. I know you have dreams—big dreams. And sometimes you doubt those dreams will come true. But doubting only brings delays, and focusing on what isn't happening brings even further delays.

HOW DO YOU KICK-START THE FABULOUS LIFE YOU WERE BORN (YES BORN!) TO LIVE? You ...

Trust you will get there.

Trust you are in the right place for right now.

Trust that your unseen friends are present and guiding you.

And know that it's not about getting there—it's about being *here*.

You see, my sweet past self, I also work with *my* future self (who might be called your "future future self"). And I've come to understand that, once we are done with this lifetime, the question won't be, "Did you accomplish much?" It will be, "Did you love much?"

So the trick, as I understand it, is to be really present and loving in each moment, while "being" the fabulous you whom you dream of being in the future.

A bit of a paradox, I know. But hey, we can do this.

I KNOW, BECAUSE I DID IT. AND YOU WILL DO IT, TOO.

I guess the bottom line is, *be* your dream. Know, in your heart of hearts, that you already have everything you've ever wanted. Because you do. Oh, you really do! It's right here, between us, connecting us, waiting for you to know it, too.

With love, love, and more love,

your future self

10

what i see in you

SOMETIMES, I'D LIKE TO JUST WRAP YOU IN MY WINGS, and protect you from everything and anything that doesn't make you happy.

On the other hand, I know who you are and what you are capable of. I've always known. And I've always been in awe.

I WISH THAT YOU COULD SEE WHAT I SEE IN YOU.

I see you as capable, strong, and powerful.

I see your love—you have such an amazing capacity to love.

I see your ability to be crystal-clear, focused, and filled with resolve.

I see your desires, and dreams filled with power, majesty, and grace.

I see you as the artist of your life, with no exceptions.

You can change your world, dear one. You can change *the* world.

And you can start by honoring, recognizing, and loving yourself. Truly.

YOU ARE WONDERFUL IN SO MANY WAYS.

Are you perfect? Never, as long as you are human. Are you perfection personified, a sliver of God and The Goddess, having an imperfectly perfect experience? Yes, you are.

Give yourself a full minute, right now, to think of all the ways in which you are perfectly wonderful. Because you are.

YOU ARE PERFECTLY HUMAN, AND PERFECTLY DIVINE, ALL AT THE SAME TIME.

It's miraculous, really.

It's time to wake up, dear one. It's time to start taking your life more seriously, and treating it as the gift it was intended to be.

And it's also time to stop taking life so seriously—to laugh, smile, and fully enjoy it.

Life is a paradox. And therein lies the triumph: let both be true.

With great love and respect for you,

your guardian angel

Bring Your "A" Game!

DO YOU WANT TO KNOW ONE SECRET TO A LONGER, HAPPIER LIFE?

I'll tell you—IT'S TO SUCK THE JUICE OUT OF LIFE.

I mean, stop sleeping through your life. Wake up! Let your senses revel in your physical and emotional experience.

For instance:

Don't just clean the house! As you do the dishes, bask in the feeling of the warm water on your hands. As you straighten the living room, take in the beauty around you. As you make the bed and do the laundry, feel the love and gratitude for the niceties of your home, and for the people who live there. Allow yourself to experience the joys of the place you reside: the comfort, the warmth, the colors, and the scents.

Don't just eat a meal with friends! Remember who they are: the living representatives of God and Goddess. Enjoy them fully. Embrace their love and your love for them. Let your senses come alive as if you were eating for the very first time. Let your surroundings, and the entire experience, be magical!

Don't just go to work! Be fully present in your body, mind, and spirit (me!) when you work. Engage fully. Remember that you have taken on a responsibility and challenge yourself to do it to the very best of your ability. Remember, and focus on what you love about it.

Bring your "A" game to your own life. And make it a "game" of doing the very best job you can, feeling and thinking and showing up as if your life depended on it.

BECAUSE MY FRIEND, YOUR LIFE *DOES* DEPEND ON IT.

No, you won't die if you do your job (or live your life) half asleep. But on the other hand, part of you *does* die when you live life halfway: ME.

Yes, when you don't live to the fullest, your spirit dies.

Act as if this were the last day of your life! Or, if you prefer, act as if this were the *first* day of your life. Live your life sensuously. Your world will respond. Just you wait.
More opportunities will present themselves. More good things will happen …

… And you will be having so much fun, you won't even care that they do. They will just be more of the same: more fun and fully-lived experiences!

The more you live your life fully alive, the more addictive it gets.

ARE YOU READY FOR IT?

I love you, my friend, and don't you forget it!

Come Out of Your Comfort Zone

WHAT WILL SNAP YOU OUT OF YOUR COMFORT ZONE, MY LOVE? Yes, I am asking you quite bluntly. What will make you take that leap into the life you dream of? Because, my love, that's what you came here to do.

You didn't plan on staying asleep.

You don't want to continue to hide.

You don't (really and truly don't) desire to stay small.

YES, IT'S TIME TO COME OUT. And no—you don't have to do it overnight. But, my love, you must stay conscious. Stay awake. You don't want this lifetime to pass you by.

Oh, I suppose in the long run, it doesn't matter. If it takes you a thousand more lifetimes to "get it," who cares, right?

Well, *I* care—not that you accomplish anything in particular, but that you're happy, that you're fulfilled, and that you have as much fun as you possibly can. Because that's what you came here to do.

I LOVE YOU. AND I WANT WHAT YOU WANT.

If you want to be sad, I don't stop you.

If you want to be a victim, it hurts my heart, but I let you.

I won't stand in your way. No matter what you believe, what you think you deserve, or what you are willing to accept. Why? Because that is the deal we made when you became physical. And I love and respect you too much to break my promise.

But my love, it *can* be easier. You can wake up, and stay awake. Life can be filled with fun, joy, love, and abundance all the time (yes, ALL the time).

YOU'VE GOT NOTHING TO LOSE, BUT A LIFE YOU ADORE TO GAIN.

So why not try? Why not dream it, commit to it, and do everything you can to make it come true? What do you have to lose, after all? Scarcity, victimhood, mediocrity?

I love you, dear one. I always have. And I always will.

Yours forever,

The Goddess

13

FROM YOUR SUBCONSCIOUS MIND

Your Present Feelings = Your Future Reality

SINCE IT'S MY JOB TO STORE EVERYTHING—ALL YOUR THOUGHTS, FEELINGS, AND EXPERIENCES OF THE PAST, AS WELL AS YOUR HOPES AND FEARS OF THE FUTURE—I REALLY SEE WHAT'S GOING ON.

And I have to say, it's like a revolving door in here lately. One minute you're thinking thoughts of dreams come true, empowerment and security—and the next thing I know, you're thinking thoughts of disappointment, powerlessness, and fear.

Now, you know this already, but I want to remind you: what you think about, you strengthen, especially when those thoughts have strong emotion attached. What you speak about, you strengthen even more.

If you want to move forward into a future of fun, abundance, and excitement, you've got to start thinking thoughts that make you feel excited, abundant, and happy—even before good things start happening.

But if you keep being reactive—seeing things "out there" and assuming they are indicative of your future—you're going to be disappointed.

JUST REMEMBER ONE THING:
YOUR PRESENT FEELINGS = YOUR FUTURE REALITY.

You really are powerful. Just look at what you've created so far. Your so-called "negative realities" are as much proof of your power as "positive" ones. The universe doesn't care which it delivers; it's just the deliveryman. You place the orders—why not order what you want?

Again, this is simply a little reminder. I know you've got this.

With love and great belief in your powers,

Your Subconscious Mind

14

FROM YOUR HIGHER SELF

YOU ARE ENOUGH

HAVE YOU EVER FELT OVERWHELMED? LIKE YOU CAN'T SEEM
TO GET IT ALL DONE? LIKE YOU AREN'T QUITE
WHO YOU REALLY WANT TO BE?

Do you ever feel as though you could be better at things? Better at being healthy? A better
friend, lover, parent, or child? More successful, more spiritual, more abundant,
more present, or more caring?

WHAT IF I WERE TO TELL YOU, "YOU ARE ABSOLUTELY ENOUGH,
RIGHT AT THIS VERY MOMENT?"

What if you were to really let this in: "You do not need to grow, or do, or be anything
more than what you are right now?"

If you accomplish nothing more than what you have accomplished, if you never love another
minute, if you never again do anything other than sit in a corner and gaze into the distance—
you are still divine. You are still holy. You are still a perfect reflection of God and Goddess.

I know that it's easy to feel as if you've fallen short. It's a side effect of your planet.

But here is the truth—you need to get off the merry-go-round before you can let the magic happen. You need to stop chasing the dream.

STOP EXPECTING PERFECTION. STOP LETTING YOUR NEGATIVE SELF TELL YOU THAT YOU MUST DO OR BE SOMETHING DIFFERENT THAN YOU ALREADY ARE.

Or, better yet, listen to your negative self tell you how you don't measure up—thus freeing yourself from its energy—and then let me take it away for healing.

THEN, JUST LET IT IN: YOU ARE ENOUGH.

Relax, and enjoy this minute, this day, this life. Feel gratitude for every little and big blessing that comes your way. Once you've set your internal anchor in freedom, peace, and love, things will start to shift in your outer world, too!

And BE.

Be in peace. Be in joy. Be in love.

Yours forevermore,

YOUR HIGHER SELF

15

FROM YOUR SOUL

Now Is The Time

IF I COULD BE PHYSICAL FOR ONLY A MOMENT, I WOULD REACH OUT AND DRAW YOU CLOSE TO ME.

I would embrace you, gently, tenderly. And I would whisper in your ear:

"Stop for a minute, my love. Stop the 'doing' in the physical world, and listen for just a moment.

"You know that the physical is not real—and yet you operate as if it is. You are simply on a training mission. Physicality is an illusion, and you are visiting the make-believe mission site. Your real home is beyond three dimensions, and your real self is beyond your personality.

"You are strong beyond measure.

"You are gifted with genius—genius, dear one!

"And you are so inherently powerful that you can create literally anything you can imagine."

Maybe, if I were physical, you would let those words in. But I can't be. These are the rules we all agreed to before we started playing this game. But, you can *imagine* me there, and that will draw me to you. I AM REAL—so imagine me physical, and let my words in deeper than you ever have before.

Because it's time now—time to get "real."

IT'S TIME TO FOLLOW YOUR HEART.

IT'S TIME TO LET YOUR TRUE SELF EMERGE, AND FINALLY LIVE THE LIFE YOU CAME HERE TO LIVE.

I believe in you. I absolutely know you can do this.

You don't need to make big changes or do it all in a day, a week, or even a year— but you will only reach your dream by moving toward it.

SO, WHAT WILL YOUR BABY STEP BE TODAY?

(And when you've identified that baby step, and taken it, get quiet for a moment, and tell me all about it. I'll be here, listening.)

With everlasting love,

Your Soul

16

YOU ARE MY FACE

YOU ARE MY FACE ON YOUR PLANET. You know that, don't you?

Yes, every one of you is my face. But you, my child, know it now.

I say this not to manipulate you into "being good," but to inspire you to realize that you are far bigger than you are currently showing yourself to be.

IT'S TIME TO STOP PLAYING SMALL, MY LOVE.

You have a destiny, a plan for this lifetime. It is not to cure cancer, or to end world hunger or to stop global warming—not by yourself, anyway. But it *is* your destiny to dream a world where those things happen.

Can you imagine a world without disease, war, or an unhealthy planet?

IF NOT YOU, THEN WHO?

Yes, you are that powerful. No, you do not have to do it alone. But you are not here by accident.

YOUR THOUGHTS MATTER. YOUR FEELINGS CREATE.

And you *can* make a difference—in your own life and in the creation of a new world.

So today, as you go about your day, imagine a world that is loving, caring, compassionate, and free, and that provides dignity for all. Imagine a world where all people—including you— laugh more than they cry, create more than they complain, and love a trillion times more than they fear.

If you can imagine it, you can create it. And what a world it will be!

I so deeply love you,

GOD

FROM YOUR FUTURE SELF

you can get here

MY LIFE IS DIFFERENT FROM YOURS in many ways. Yes, your dreams (and then some) have come true—I am living proof. Soon, you will dream dreams you can't even imagine—and many of those will come true as well.

But the real difference between you and I is the *peace*. I am so very peaceful. You see, I discovered that worry, impatience, and fear don't produce realities I like— and I AM CREATING MY REALITY ALL OF THE TIME.

I've come to trust that creation process. Now, I know that no matter what happens in my world, I will be fine. More than fine: I will triumph. That knowing—that absolute knowing—brings me peace.

And OMG, beyond being peaceful, my life is so much fun! You can't get to fun and peace (not to mention prosperity and love) by dwelling on the past and feeling like a failure. You just can't. But I know you can get *here*, because I did—and I am you!

Yours in joy, fun, and love,

your future self

it's your illusion

IT SEEMS PRETTY FAR AWAY SOMETIMES, DOESN'T IT— WHERE YOU ARE, FROM WHERE YOU WANT TO BE?

Sometimes it feels like an uphill battle. And sometimes it feels as though you don't have the support you'd like or need.

I know, dear one. I know.

But, here's the thing: this world is an illusion, and it's *your* illusion, completely and totally. I know it would be easier if you could just point to someone or something "out there" as the cause of your problems.

BUT, MY DEAR, IT ALWAYS COMES BACK TO YOU.

And that is good news.

Nothing has to be a struggle. Everything can go smoothly—magically even—if you just let go and trust that you will get there. Just remember that every obstacle and opposition you come across is a whisper that you are not fully in alignment with your dream.

Love the obstacles for pointing out where you can
love yourself more.

Accept the struggle with compassion for yourself and your journey,
and resolve to allow more ease and elegance.

Let your reality show you where your beliefs should be replaced, in order to
truly live the life of your dreams.

And RAISE YOUR RESONANCE TO THE POINT WHERE OPPOSITION IS
NON-EXISTENT, and your life is just one magical, fun synchronicity after the next.

(Yes, it is possible!)

You can do this, dearest one. It's what you came to do.

With so much love,

your guardian angel

19

It's SO Exciting!

DOESN'T IT FEEL GREAT TO BE EXCITED?

When you are excited, I come alive!

Excitement is the best feeling ever (besides love, that is). And the cool thing is, excitement produces more excitement. Passion produces more passion. In fact, feeling *anything* invites more of the same feeling!

Now THAT rocks.

But sometimes it's not so easy to feel excited, is it? Sometimes you wish you could feel excited, or passionate, but it just isn't there. (Hey, I've been observing.)

Here's the thing though: YOU ARE THE ONE WITH THE POWER. You are the one who chooses. You are the one who can change everything. Seriously. *You are creating it all.* If you really let that in, and I mean really—there is no way you could not live every moment of your life totally jazzed!

So, how do you start to create that change?

TRY MOVEMENT.

Move your body! Find some really fun, uplifting music and dance it out.

Move your mind! Stretch the limits of your imagination. How crazy, wildly great could your life be? Read books that stretch your concept of the possible.

Move your life! Switch something up—even if it's just taking a new route home from work and seeing the world with new eyes. Say hello to a stranger. Do something loving for someone who doesn't expect it.

Start small if you have to, but move with the intention of becoming more excited about life.

You see, status quo produces status quo. EVEN A TINY BIT OF EXCITEMENT, IF YOU FEED IT, WILL PRODUCE MORE AND MORE AND MORE.

At the very least, allow yourself to get excited about the idea of more excitement in your life!

I love you—to the moon and back!

FROM THE GODDESS

Let Go of The Fear

YOU FEEL THINGS CHANGING, DON'T YOU?

Sometimes it's exciting, and you can't wait for each new day. Sometimes it's petrifying, and you wish you had your old world back.

I understand, my love. I feel your excitement and your fear.

It's okay to have both. I *expect* you to have both. But know this: THE FEAR BELONGS TO AN "OLD YOU"—YOUR PAST SELF. You are not that person any more, but you can have compassion for that part of you, because this fear *is* real to that old you.

I suggest sitting with your fearful self. Let it run wild with stories of doom and gloom. Listen to it. Let it play out for you the very worst-case scenarios. And then take that fear—all of it— place it in a bubble of light, and watch it float away.

Assure the fearful you that you do, indeed, have it handled. And let it go off in peace.

MEANWHILE, IMAGINE YOUR WILDEST DREAMS WITHOUT THE BURDEN OF FEAR.

Will this eliminate your fear forever and completely? Likely not. But it will free you—for a while—to soar. And your soaring excitement is exponentially more powerful than your very worst fears.

I do love you so. The depth of love I have for you is immeasurable, inconceivable, and inexpressible. It is here for you to bask in, to become stronger in, and to find peace in, any time you desire. Simply think of me, and ask to feel my love.

Always and forever,

The Goddess

21

FROM YOUR SUBCONSCIOUS MIND

Time For An Update

Whether you know it or not, I keep things very tidy in your world.
There are no inconsistencies here.

I OPERATE LIKE A COMPUTER. BELIEFS IN = REALITIES OUT.

Each and every belief you put into me, you will see reflected back in your reality.

I don't get rid of anything, either; I still remember what you had for breakfast on May 25 of the year you were four. But I do want you to know that we have quite a few old, outdated beliefs up here. Maybe it's time to update and replace a few of them?

(Just saying.)

Yours faithfully,

Your Subconscious Mind

FROM YOUR HIGHER SELF

HEALING YOUR CHILD SELF

DO YOU REMEMBER WHEN YOU WERE SIX OR SEVEN YEARS OLD?

There were some scary times for that little you. Yes, you've grown up and moved on—but that little you still exists. That little you still gets scared and feels inadequate.

But you can help.

Tonight, before you go to sleep, imagine yourself sneaking into that little one's room, crawling into bed with them, and cradling them in your love.

Whisper in their ear:

"I love you. I love you deeply. I love you unconditionally—just the way you are. You are perfect, in my eyes, and I will love you forever and always."

Then, imagine surrounding that little one in a bubble of white, sparkling light, so they will feel that love and acceptance far into the night and throughout the next day.

You are powerful. You can heal that little one with your intention and your love.

AND WHEN THE CHILD "YOU" HEALS, SO DO YOU.

With deep, abiding love,

YOUR HIGHER SELF

PS: Tonight, after you've loved your little self to sleep, imagine me sneaking into your room, crawling into bed with you, and wrapping you in my love. I will whisper in your ear, *"I love you. I love you deeply. I love you unconditionally—just the way you are. You are perfect, in my eyes, and I will love you forever and always."* I will then wrap you in a bubble of white sparkling light, and you will feel my love and healing far into the night and throughout the next day.

23

FROM YOUR SOUL

Your "Almost" Dreams

DO YOU REALIZE HOW MANY OF YOUR DREAMS HAVE *ALMOST* MANIFESTED? Dreams you allowed yourself to dream, but then pulled back on. Dreams you didn't think you were good enough for. Dreams you were so impatient for that you pushed them away.

There are quite a few of these "almost dreams," my love.

And this is fine. You are on this planet to learn to manifest your dreams, so of course you have a few that have fallen short.

But what I want you to realize is that THERE IS NOTHING "OUT THERE" THAT HAS PREVENTED YOUR DREAMS FROM MANIFESTING. The reason they haven't come true is *you*. It is always you.

You are reading this today because you are ready, more than ever before, to take responsibility for your thoughts, feelings, and beliefs, and create those dreams you hold so dear—even the "almost" dreams that belong to earlier versions of you.

Dreams take time because you set it up this way. Time lag (the time between your energy and your manifestation) gives you ample opportunity to fall short without suffering.

YOU ARE GOOD ENOUGH. You can learn patience, and hold hope in your heart. So, go back to one of those "almost dreams" that didn't manifest—that thing you wanted but didn't receive—and give your past self that dream. That's right: go into meditation, and give your past self what they wanted. Feel their joy, their excitement, their belief in themselves (and you). Do this for all of the past "yous" who suffered disappointments, betrayals, and hurts.

THEN, BRING THAT FEELING BACK TO THE PRESENT, AND START DREAMING YOUR CURRENT DREAMS—because your energy is now freed up to manifest in the here and now.

Be patient, my love. You are far more powerful than you realize.

With unending love,

Your Soul

24

YOU ARE DESERVING

I LOVE YOU SO DEEPLY, AND SO UNCONDITIONALLY, that you would weep, could you let in even the tiniest bit of that love.

You don't have to earn my love. You don't have to live up to my love.

In fact, you don't have to do anything.

Well, actually, my child, there is one thing I'd like you to do for me—not to earn my love, that is a given—but as a favor to me.

I'D REALLY LOVE IT IF YOU COULD LOVE YOURSELF
WITHOUT CONDITION, TOO.

You do a good job of loving me and your other unseen friends without condition. You don't base your love and acceptance on how much we weigh, what we look like, how well we do at a given task, what our job status is, or any other arbitrary measurement.

You just love us.

And I'd love it if you'd just love you the same way—without condition. Because like it or not, accept it or not, you *are* us.

YOU ARE DIVINE. AND YOU ARE DESERVING OF UNLIMITED, UNCONDITIONAL LOVE.

Let go of the old stories about who you are, and what's "wrong" with you. Forgive the past, because it's over and done with. Today can be a brand new start to a brand new life.

I would be thrilled to help you with this. You only need to ask, child, and I will be there.

The really wonderful side effect of loving yourself as I love you is that it will make creating your reality on Earth so much easier and more elegant. Synchronicities and opportunities will abound, offering new levels of success, joy, fun, and abundance.

You are deserving of that, too. And I would love to see you create it.

With deep and profound love,

GOD

25

FROM YOUR FUTURE SELF

i am pulling you toward me

HAVE I TOLD YOU HOW MUCH I LOVE MY LIFE?

I'm smiling as I write that, because I'm sure I have. And yet, I have to say it again. I am *soooooo* happy. And I'm at peace, too. Oh, and excited: I cannot wait for the sun to come up every morning because life is just so darn much fun!

Yes, your story really does have a happy ending (or beginning, depending upon how you look at it). AND YOU—WE—MADE IT HAPPEN.

I know you aren't quite here yet. That's why I like to check in with you, and remind you about things you may have forgotten. One of those things is your *image*.

I know that you don't always think of yourself as the powerful, together, gorgeous, smart, successful, spiritual babe that you are. In fact, who are we kidding: sometimes you are pretty hard on yourself.

I GOTTA TELL YOU, THAT JUST WON'T GET YOU HERE.

Things really began to change for me when I gave up feeling that I didn't do it right, did it too slow, or just plain failed.

It's funny, because always thinking you could have done better is a habit.

On the flip side, so is thinking you are right on track. Because, kiddo, you are.

Yes, you *are* doing it right. You *haven't* let anyone down.
You *can* forgive yourself for all of your perceived shortcomings.

And you can know you are enough. You are *divine*. You deserve a fabulous, delicious, exciting, abundant, prosperous, and love-filled life.

THIS IS YOUR ILLUSION. WHY NOT GET WHAT YOU REALLY WANT?

With love, love, love,

your future self

PS: I am pulling you towards me. Can you feel it?

26

FROM YOUR GUARDIAN ANGEL

you are going to be okay

LIFE CAN GET SCARY, DEAR ONE. I know that.
I see it in your world: the threats to safety, freedom, and the future.

Whether your current fear is for a future you are afraid won't manifest, for a loved one who is in pain, or for the world itself and the atrocities it faces each day, I want you to know:

IT'S OKAY.

You're going to be okay. Your loved ones are going to be okay.
And the world is going to be okay, too.

You see, fear is going to come up for you in this illusion, because the only thing certain here (besides the fact that you are divine) is *change*. And change tends to be accompanied by fear.

The unknown scares humans, especially when you forget that this is an illusion. You forget that you can choose the outcome of the changes. You forget that you are a powerful reality creator.

IT'S OKAY TO FEEL AFRAID. BUT PLEASE, FEEL IT DEEPLY AND FULLY, AND THEN LET IT GO AND BE DONE WITH IT.

Only when you let go of the fear can you move into the power and authority that you were born to express with ownership, conviction, and faith. Once you've done that, you can feel the essence you choose to exist within: safety, trust, empowerment, and peace.

That is the secret to transmuting fear.

If you have trouble letting go of the fear, call on me. I will be with you. I will hold you as you feel the fear, and bolster you as you let it move through you, and out of you.

Then, I will join you as you move into the essence you prefer, and assist you in maintaining that essence, day after day.

With tremendous love and respect,

your guardian angel

27

FROM YOUR SPIRIT

You Are So Lucky!

It is SO exciting, isn't it, this illusion humans call "life?"

I mean, come *on*: three dimensions (with that bonus dimension—Time!) all rolled together for your enjoyment, giving your illusion depth, breadth, color, and light!

What's more, your illusionary playground is the super gorgeous planet you call Earth— and, on top of that, you get to create everything that happens to you while you're there.

WOW, YOU ARE SO LUCKY!

What's that? You're not feeling quite as excited about this as I am?

I have noticed that it's easy for you to get sidetracked and slip into overwhelm with all that pulls at your attention on this planet. But you don't have to react to what is happening around you. In fact, if you do, you are giving up your considerable power.

Instead, be proactive.

For instance, a day in your time dimension has 24 hours in it, correct? Well, it's obvious that you won't be able to do everything that is in your head in those 24 hours. When you try, what generally happens is you feel you have to hurry, or multi-task, or give up some of the things you want to do. You end up feeling overwhelmed and inadequate. You then go "unconscious" and begin to do things you never even really wanted to do—like zoning out over some TV show or web page or whatever.

HERE'S HOW TO CHANGE THAT:

Make a list of everything you want to do each day. Prioritize each item by importance, and only do the things you really want to do. (Ideally, only do the things you *love* to do.) Then, do every single one of those things with as much joy, focus, love, and excitement as you can.

You can also make that list for your whole life. What is it that you want to do with your life? What do you want to create? Prioritize that list, and add a piece a day to your daily list.

BABY STEPS WILL GET YA THERE, BABY!

This is your illusion, and you're creating every second of it. So stop giving your time and attention (aka your energy and power) to what you don't want. Instead, give it to the things you do want—and soon, you'll be soaring every single day, just like me!

With a crazy amount of love,

Your Spirit ♡♥

28

FROM THE GODDESS

Now Is All There Is

BE STILL, MY LOVE, FOR I HAVE AN IMPORTANT MESSAGE FOR YOU.

I've noticed that you aren't as blissful as you could be. Oh, yes, you are happy—but you could be happier, couldn't you? You could be *blissfully* happy with your life.

"How," you ask?

BY SLOWING DOWN.

By allowing each and every moment you live to be a divine reflection of you, and by honoring it as you honor yourself.

You can live your divinity by *remembering*, my love. Remember why you are in a physical body in the first place. You are only here temporarily, until you return home, and this sojourn is meant to be a beautiful, sensuous, extraordinary gift.

When you finally accept your reality for the gift it is, and cherish all the wonderful things about it, you will begin to see changes in your world.

IT IS A PARADOX, ISN'T IT? YOU HAVE TO SEE THE BEAUTY
IN YOUR WORLD BEFORE MORE BEAUTY APPEARS.

But paradox or not, it is the way it works. Look around you. Life is good. You have love. You have beauty. You have a level of abundance. You have a depth of knowing about who you are. And your life is getting better—as is the world.

SO, LIVE THE LIFE YOU WERE MEANT TO LIVE.
NOW. TODAY. THIS VERY MINUTE!

You don't have to wait. You can live who you want to be *now*. You can claim joy *now*. You can feel abundant *now*. You can live in the moment *now*—extracting every succulent bit of juiciness that you can from this very instant.

Because, as you and I both know, *now* is all there is.

With the deepest love possible,

The Goddess

Clean Out The Files

My, we have been creating some interesting realities lately haven't we?

The good news is, realities are manifesting quicker these days.
The bad news is, realities are manifesting quicker these days.

YOUR BELIEFS (STORED HERE WITH ME, SECURELY AND SAFELY) WILL ALWAYS PRODUCE YOUR REALITY. That will never change.

But *you* have changed. You have learned so much, and you are more willing than ever to do what is necessary to change your life (not to mention the lives of others and the world).

I hold your memories for you throughout your entire lifetime. Why, I still have memories from when you were three years old! I also have every limiting belief, every belief about drama and struggle and mediocrity, that you've ever believed. And believe me, you've had enough of these things to last a lifetime!

You have the keys to come in, anytime you like, and clean out my filing cabinets. You can replace your old, limiting beliefs with beautiful, success-allowing, love-creating, possibility-producing beliefs.

SO, LET'S FILL THOSE FILES WITH SOMETHING MORE EXPANSIVE, SHALL WE? (I know that Lonnsburry woman writes a lot about how to do exactly that!)

Once you open the door, I'll do what I can to help—and so will all of your other unseen friends. We all want your life to be spectacular.

So let's do it, O Powerful Human! Let's schedule some time in your calendar. Clear an hour or two, right now. Pretend that this is the most important thing in your life—because it is!

With love,

Your Subconscious Mind

30

FROM YOUR HIGHER SELF

I AM PROUD OF YOU

DO YOU HAVE ANY IDEA HOW PROUD I AM OF YOU?

I'm really, truly honored to be your higher self.

You came to a planet where you knew you would be challenged to be who you really are—
a planet where so many are still asleep. You faced the challenge head-on, and,
despite the rocky road, you have persevered.

And not only have you persevered, you've come a *long* way. Every step forward you take, you
leave a footprint for others to follow. You make a map for an entire humanity to wake up and
see the truth—that each and every one of you is a god-being, gifted with a universe
that responds to your will.

You don't do everything perfectly. I know that. But don't you see? THE WHOLE IDEA OF
BEING HUMAN IS TO BE UNABASHEDLY WILLING TO MAKE MISTAKES.
It was set up this way, so that mistakes would be part of the learning process, and
forgiveness would be a necessary key to evolve.

Speaking of forgiveness … How are you doing on that front? Have you fully forgiven yourself for all of your mistakes, conscious and unconscious? Have you forgiven yourself for not being "further ahead" than you currently are? (Yes, I know you well.)

DEAREST ONE, FREEDOM IS HIDDEN WITHIN FORGIVENESS.

When you forgive, you unlock the shackles that keep you bound to the past, and to reliving old "mistakes" over and over again.

I love you so deeply—deeper than you can even imagine. And I want you to be free to live the life you came here to live.

Call upon me to help, please? I'm here for you, for whatever your heart desires.

With inexhaustible love,

YOUR HIGHER SELF

31

FROM YOUR SOUL

Finding Your Destiny

I KNOW YOU DON'T REMEMBER OUR MEETINGS BEFORE YOU BECAME PHYSICAL IN THIS LIFETIME—but we had them. Many of them.

We meticulously planned the energies you would incarnate with. We planned your strengths and your weaknesses. We planned your challenges, and the ways in which you would overcome them. And we planned your destiny.

AH, THAT WORD GOT YOUR ATTENTION, DIDN'T IT? DESTINY.

Of course you have a destiny (I know you sometimes wonder about that). How do you tell if you're living your destiny? Simple. Ask yourself these questions:

Am I doing what excites me as much as I possibly can?
Am I enjoying each and every "now" moment as fully as possible?
Am I listening to that quiet voice inside of me for direction and guidance?

YOU WERE BORN WITH AN INTERNAL GUIDANCE SYSTEM THAT WILL ABSOLUTELY UNFOLD YOUR DESTINY—*IF* YOU FOLLOW IT.

What does your destiny look like? It might not be winning the next Pulitzer Prize, or discovering the answer to the world's energy crisis. It might not be becoming famous. But your destiny is the life path that makes you the happiest, and utilizes your talents and skills to the highest possible level—and it is the path by which you can make the greatest possible difference in the world.

One thing I want you to remember: MAKING A DIFFERENCE IN THE WORLD DOESN'T ALWAYS SHOW UP VISIBLY IN THE WORLD. But I promise that your energy of excitement, love, compassion, and joy will be the catalyst for others to seek their own joy—and through them, for still others to seek theirs. Just by following your inner voice, you can create a wave of people bringing their greatest gifts to the planet. You may never know who those people are, but it doesn't matter, because your destiny doesn't include your ego. It can't. Your ego is part of what makes you human, but your destiny is divinely mandated.

So go forth, knowing that all you have to do to be your best self and find your destiny is to have fun, stay present, and listen for my voice guiding you along the way. Trust that every twist and turn has a purpose that you will understand someday. Stay aligned with the three questions above, and someday we will look back on your life and see just how perfectly the path unfolded.

With colossal love,

Your Soul

MY JOB IS TO LOVE YOU

Some would say I have a tough job.

MY JOB IS TO LOVE YOU WITH ALL MY HEART,
AND THEN LET YOU GO.

My job is to want your happiness so badly I can taste it—but then let you make your own mistakes, even if those mistakes result in some temporary unhappiness.

My job is to let you "do it for yourself," even though I could do it for you, because I honor your choice to practice creating here in the illusion called Earth.

I say I have an easy job.

I GET TO LOVE YOU. HOW MUCH MORE WONDERFUL DOES IT GET?

I get to support and guide you. Believe me, there is hardly a more rewarding occupation.

I get to watch you grow. Something that makes me smile just thinking about it.

I get to watch you have fun. I wish I could do this more often—but when you do allow your life to be playful and sweet, it warms my heart deeply, because "fun" is the way that life is meant to be.

I get to watch you love. Oh, my, how you do love. Maybe not when you are angry, or sad, or afraid (you are human after all), but your ability to love is truly amazing.

I AM HONORED THAT YOU ARE A PART OF ME, DEAREST ONE.
Thank you for your choice to play the game of Earth. Because as you grow and become more, I grow and become more, as does everything else in the multiverse.

I love you, forever and beyond,

GOD

33

change is happening

IT'S EASY TO LOSE MOMENTUM, ISN'T IT?

How do I know this? I've been there, remember?

I remember looking out over my life and wondering, "Just when is everything going to change? I'm doing the work, but my reality doesn't always happen the way I want it to!"

That one thought was the thought that made my creations lose momentum.

Oh, how I wish I knew then what I know now ...

WAIT A MINUTE—by writing this to you, I DO know then what I know now! How cool is that?

Anyway, let me continue ...

If you look over the past five or ten years, you'll notice your reality *did* change, and you *did* grow. You just didn't always feel it at the time.

Change happens quickly, without your noticing, so having faith that things will change is ever so important.

THE MINUTE YOU BEGIN TO LAMENT THAT NOT ENOUGH IS CHANGING, YOUR REALITIES TURN AND GO THE OTHER WAY.

A critical thing to remember, dear past self, is that the universe ebbs and flows. It always has, and it always will. During the "ebbs," it is most self-loving to accept the lull as a beautiful space of respite, to relax, ponder, dream, and rejuvenate.

I guess what I'm trying to say is: TRUST THE TIMING. Divine timing really is divine. Be gentle with yourself around creating. If you have beliefs you suspect need to change, by all means, change them. But once you have, and once you've done your daily technique, let it go—and trust. That is conscious creating at its finest.

With love forever,

your future self

34

keep making the choice

I'M HERE FOR YOU, YOU KNOW.

I realize sometimes I seem like a fantasy to you—rather than a real, live being who knows you and loves you without condition. But I'm not a fantasy.

I.

AM.

REAL.

And I really love you.

I also see you. Oh, not literally, I don't spy on you. But I see your energy. I feel your sadness and your joy—your excitement and your disappointment.

AND RIGHT NOW, I FEEL YOUR HOPE.

You feel it too, don't you—the possibility that everything can be different now?

Oh, maybe you're afraid to even admit it. After all, you've hoped things could be different before, and you were disappointed with the way things turned out.

But this really does feel different, doesn't it?

THAT'S BECAUSE YOU *ARE* DIFFERENT.

So don't shut it down—this energy of hope and anticipation and excitement. Don't let your negative self tell you lies, like: "Oh, nothing has really changed ... Don't get your hopes up, kiddo ... You're bound to be disappointed if you do."

Because *this* is the time your negative self always pipes up: just before the magic happens.

SO, STAY DETERMINED: to hold onto the glimmers of hope, grab the threads of excitement, and anticipate living a life filled with peace, joy, love, and prosperity.
You have the power. You have the ability.

NOW, MAKE THE CHOICE. AND KEEP MAKING THAT CHOICE, AGAIN AND AGAIN, AS MANY TIMES AS YOU NEED TO.

Because it's that choice, dear one—that determination to let nothing stop you—that will continue to change everything.

With deep and abiding love,

your guardian angel

Your Spirit, Reborn!

HAVE YOU NOTICED THAT I'VE GOTTEN SMALLER OVER THE YEARS?
Have you noticed that you're feeling less passionate and excited than you did
when you were an adolescent or a young adult?

WHAT HAPPENED TO THAT JUICE, FRIEND?

I know one thing that has happened to it: you've left it behind after each and every
disappointment in your life.

Each time a dream of yours was dashed, a little piece of me was left behind with that dream.
Every time you were disappointed, hurt, betrayed, abandoned, or had to settle, a piece of me
died—and a piece of your passion, excitement, and exuberance died as well.

Yes, it is sad. But there is hope.

You can revive that lost passion. You can rekindle the enthusiasm and
reignite your spark of excitement about life!

Here's how you can start:

Make a list of the biggest disappointments of your life. Then, go back (in meditation) to each and every one of those times, and visit the "you" before the disappointment happened.

And then—here's the key—CHANGE THE OUTCOME!

Yes, that's right. Give that "you" the dream they wanted. Don't judge it. Don't second-guess it. Just give that you what you were hoping for, in spades. Watch that old you become *so* excited as their dreams come true. Be happy for them (even if what they wanted is not even close to your current dream).

And then come back to full consciousness, and do it again for every past you who didn't get what they wanted.

VOILA! YOUR SPIRIT SHALL BE REBORN.

How cool is that, eh?

With oceans of love,

Your Spirit ☺

36

Divine Timing

Sometimes it's hard for you to connect with me. Sometimes it's hard for you to hear me through all the noise of your world (not to mention the noise in your head).

BUT I'M HERE. I'M ALWAYS HERE FOR YOU, MY LOVE.

And if you'll be still—if you'll be quiet—and allow me to wrap my arms of light around you, I will.

Just say, *"Goddess, please be with me. Touch me. Love me. Help me to see clearly and act lovingly."*

Or, say something else that communicates what you desire. Whatever it is, I'll be there. I'm always there for you. I am always ready to connect with you, to touch you and to love you. I don't always have a message for you, though (although sometimes I do). Sometimes it is most appropriate for us to just be together.

You see, there is something called "divine timing". Divine timing is understanding, and being at peace with, the idea that there is a time for everything.

THERE IS A TIME FOR GROWTH, AND A TIME TO INTEGRATE THAT GROWTH. There is a time to manifest in your world, and a time to enjoy the results of that manifesting. And there is a time to move closer to me, and a time to revel in the relationship we currently have.

How do you tell where you are in divine timing? Simple. Listen to your heart.

YOUR HEART ALWAYS KNOWS, MY LOVE. ALWAYS.

So let's be together, shall we?

With great love,

The Goddess

You Are The Magician

I've been talking to some other subconscious minds (yes, we talk).

IT SEEMS THAT YOU CONSCIOUS MINDS TEND TO GET INTO RUTS.

You believe the same old things, year after year after year. And guess what? You create the same old realities, year after year after year.

My question is, when is it gonna change for us?

YOU COULD TAKE FIVE MINUTES, RIGHT NOW, AND
ROCK YOUR WORLD!

Come on in here, and change the belief that says, "I can't have it all." Change the belief that says, "Miracles don't happen to me." And while you're there, change the belief that says, "It's hard to create my dreams coming true!"

Don't you get it? Your world is just smoke and mirrors. And you are the magician creating the illusion. So let's create a crazy-awesome dream, okay?

LET'S GO, RIGHT HERE AND NOW.

What is the most amazing dream you can imagine?
That's right—sttttreeeeettcccchhhh your imagination!

Now, what came up for you? What was the little voice in your head saying?

"Don't be silly."

"It can't be that great?"

"Baby, you are fooling yourself!"

That little voice is pointing out your beliefs. ANYTHING is possible.
Anything at all—as long as you believe it is.

We've got some work to do! I hope you are as excited as I am!

With love and support (always),

Your Subconscious Mind

PS: I can't wait to tell the other subconscious minds about what we create together!

EXPAND YOUR GRATITUDE

You live in a magical universe capable of creating the most phenomenal life you can imagine.

I want to tell you about a powerful energy which can help you to create that extraordinary life:

GRATITUDE.

Gratitude is amazing. The more you acknowledge even the littlest gifts in your current life, the easier it will be to create an even more wonderful life.

GRATITUDE CREATES MORE TO BE GRATEFUL FOR.
It's as simple as that: the law of attraction at work.

And you have SO much to be grateful for: eyes to read this message with, a device in your hand (paper or electronic) that delivers this message, and a brain able to decipher its meaning, to name just a few.

IF YOU MAKE GRATITUDE A HABIT, SO MUCH CAN CHANGE IN YOUR WORLD.

Begin today. Start the day—either right before you jump out of bed, over breakfast, or in the shower—with a list (mental or physical) of all you are grateful for. Allow it to cover everything in your life, from the beauty you see, to the people you love, to the abundance you already have.

Be as detailed as you can. Details open your heart, and stop you from becoming automatic with gratitude. When you explore the details, the impact will be much more profound.

EXPAND YOUR GRATITUDE, AND YOU'LL EXPAND YOUR JOY, LOVE, PROSPERITY, AND ABUNDANCE.

With love and blessings,

YOUR HIGHER SELF

PS: I am grateful for *you*. It is through your eyes that I experience the world. And it is my relationship with you that brings me such profound joy. Thank *you* for being.

Dream The Big Dream

IT'S TIME NOW.

You know it. And I know it.

It's time to let go of the old stories—the stories of who you are and what your life can be like. It's time to stop pretending you are not powerful. And it's time to stretch into futures you didn't dare to dream just a few months ago.

Oh, I know you've toyed with the BIG dream here and there. The one where your life is exactly how you want it to be. But you haven't quite let it be a real possibility, have you?

Well not only is it possible, it IS going to happen.

How? YOU AND I ARE GOING TO MAKE IT HAPPEN, OF COURSE!

You still want it, don't you? It is, after all, *your* choice. But for heaven's sake, why *wouldn't* you want the big dream? Your reality is all just a dream anyway— so why not dream up the best life possible?

Your job is to get excited about this new life of yours. And when thoughts come in that put doubts in your mind, realize that that is your "negative self" talking, and gently send them on their way.

MY JOB WILL BE TO SUPPORT YOU, AND HELP YOU DISCOVER THE BELIEFS THAT STAND IN YOUR WAY. Now, I can't talk to you directly, but I can talk to you in meditation or during your times of solitude. I can also send you little messages here and there. You'll have to pay attention to hear me, though.

I am so excited for you, my love. Your life is going to be amazing!

With deepest love,

Your Soul

PS: I forgot to mention, you do need to ask me to help before I can really be of assistance. Every night, before bed, invite me to work with you in your dreams. And in the mornings, you will be a tiny bit closer to creating that fabulous life of yours!

40

FROM GOD

I AM HERE TO ASSIST YOU

I WOULD LIKE YOU TO GET TO KNOW ME BETTER.

You see, *I know you*, inside and out. Oh, I know sometimes you would prefer I didn't know you. There are some things you do that you'd rather I didn't see.

But, my child, there is nothing you could do or say or be
that would make me love you less. Nothing.

NO MATTER WHAT YOU DO—I DON'T JUDGE YOU—EVER.
My love for you is unconditional. Always.

Oh, I wish I could cradle you in my arms and tenderly hold you. I would banish all your fears with the knowledge that everything you are afraid of is merely an illusion. I would invite you to see your beauty, grace, and divinity.

But I know these are discoveries that you want to make on your own. And so I will not rob you of your chosen experience.

I will remind you of the unimaginable depths of love I have for you. And I will remind you, dear heart, that I am here to do more than love you—I am here to assist you.

WHEN YOU ARE READY, ALL YOU HAVE TO DO IS ASK.

When you do, I will guide you. I will whisper in your ear. I will speak to your heart. But you will have to listen carefully to hear me. You will have to be still and listen to that silent voice within you. Because that voice is me.

With all my love,

GOD

41

let go of the past

If you knew what you are capable of, you'd never worry another day in your life.

THERE IS ABSOLUTELY NOTHING YOU CAN'T HAVE, OR DO, OR BE.

NOTHING.

But the trick is, you need to *own* that at every level of your being. You need to *be* that person who has what you want, and who *is* what you want, right now.

BASICALLY YOU NEED TO BE *ME*, RIGHT NOW.

And what fun that will be for you! I know because I AM me.
(This does get a little complex doesn't it?)

Oh, past self, I guess what I'm trying to say is that I am living a phenomenal life! I don't have a worry in the world. I adore every minute I am alive. I am filled with passion for my work and for life. Abundance is everywhere I look. And I feel so very, very loved.

YOU WILL HAVE THIS LIFE TOO!

You can have it now. You can have it *emotionally*.

And if you do, you'll have it physically before you know it.

But in order to make this happen, you need to let go of the past. Let go of the failures.
Let go of the old stories of who you are, and who you can (or can't) be.
Forgive yourself for all of the mis-creations.

If you're not sure where to begin with self-forgiveness, set an intention to forgive yourself and let the past die. You can always ask our higher self for help!

If you sincerely forgive yourself, it will open the doors to a new you—
and this "you" can be anyone you want.

(Make it be me!)

With love and laughter,

your (astonishingly successful) future self

42

trust

I am here to protect you, love you, and guide you.
And if I could impart only one gift to you, it would be this:

TRUST.

Trust that you are on the right path. You are doing splendidly.
You are in the right place at the right time.

TRUST, dear one, that everything is progressing beautifully. You are on track.
You are learning at the perfect pace for you.

IF YOU STRENGTHEN YOUR TRUST, EVERYTHING WILL BECOME EASIER.

You see, there is no timetable. No hurry. You can't miss anything.

THE UNIVERSE CAN AND WILL SUPPORT ANYTHING YOU WANT.

If you worry, the universe gives you more to worry about. If you relax and believe that
everything is unfolding perfectly, you create magical synchronicities.

SO WHY NOT RELAX, AND TRUST?

Trust that there is no such thing as "luck" (bad or good). Remember that you create your world, 100%. Trust that you will be given what you need when you need it, and that your unseen friends will help you every step of the way.

Dearest one, it's easy to slip into trying to control your world when you forget that there is no need for control, but ...

CONTROL IS JUST ANOTHER WORD FOR LACK OF TRUST.

Whenever you are tempted to worry or try to control, repeat these words:
"I expect magic to happen!" I promise, it will.

I love you deeply,

your guardian angel

Are You Enjoying Your Life?

It's great to connect with you again! It's always fun to be able to communicate with you so directly. Usually I have to whisper and wait (and wait) until you are listening.

If you don't mind me saying so, sometimes that takes a *loooooong* time. This is easier.

ARE YOU ENJOYING THE HECK OUT OF YOUR LIFE, MY HUMAN SELF?

What? Not always? Why the heck not?

I don't want to tell you what to do—but we are a team, know what I mean?

And LIFE IS SUPPOSED TO BE FUN!

Oh yeah, I know yours isn't totally fun—yet. But the way you make your life totally fun is to start making every moment fun, *intending* to have fun, and changing the beliefs that say it can't be totally fun.

FUN MAKES ME COME ALIVE! Fun and passion: that is what gets me (and you) out of bed in the morning. It's what gets us excited about the day.

AND SPEAKING OF PASSION—HOW ABOUT A LITTLE MORE OF THAT IN YOUR LIFE AS WELL?

Not feeling passionate? Again, why the heck not? Passion doesn't always come knocking at your door, you know. Sometimes you have to seek it out.

Tell you what. Why don't you make a list of ten fun things you like to do, and ten things you are passionate about—just to get you started. You might be surprised where they will take you.

Then, just for giggles, DO the things on your list!

Remember, you create it all—so let's create LOTS of passion and fun, okay?

With love, love, love, and light,

44

FROM THE GODDESS

Count Your Blessings

WHAT ARE YOU CREATING TODAY, MY LOVE?

Yes, I mean that very literally. What are you creating today?

What are you paying attention to—what you desire, or what you fear? What are you feeling—joy or sadness? What are you thinking about—possibilities and exciting futures, or ho-hum drudgery?

ARE YOU COUNTING YOUR BLESSINGS, AND LISTING ALL YOU ARE GRATEFUL FOR, OR COUNTING YOUR BURDENS?

It's easy to get caught up in negativity, isn't it? And it's easy to forget that you, my love, are a powerful being.

I love you deeply. And although I will love you no matter what sort of life you choose to create, I would love to see you create a beautiful life, a prosperous life, a love-filled life.

AND YOU CAN. YOU KNOW YOU CAN.

SO FORGIVE YOURSELF FOR YOUR PAST, BEGIN TO DREAM YOUR FUTURE, AND ENJOY THIS DAY.

I have some ideas on healing, ease, and elegance; I'll whisper them in your ear, if you grant me permission.

I would love to help you, my love.

With unconditional love for you,

The Goddess

Your Self-Image Room

It is my job to store information for you—information like beliefs, patterns, habits, attitudes, etc. It is not my job to give you advice.

However, I HAVE NOTICED THAT YOU ARE CHANGING. You are no longer content to sit around and wait to see what life brings you. You are dreaming bigger dreams, and you have more desire than ever to make those dreams come true.

And because I see you want more success, abundance, love, and joy, I have a suggestion:

YOU COULD SPRUCE UP SOME THINGS HERE IN YOUR
SUBCONSCIOUS MIND.

You may not realize this, but you have a Self-Image Room that could use some work. This is the room that stores all of your ideas and beliefs about who you are—and it's a little dusty and dilapidated right now. The furniture in it looks like it's from the Salvation Army Thrift Store. It looks like it hasn't been cleaned in years—and quite honestly, if you want to manifest some of those dreams you keep thinking about, I'd suggest that you make the room quite a bit bigger than it currently is.

I'm sure you're wondering just how to go about this, right?

Well, conscious self, it's easier than you might think to change your image. Simply shut your eyes and imagine walking in nature. Suddenly, you come upon a strange thing—a staircase, right there in the middle of a forest.

And then you climb this staircase—up into the clouds. When you reach the top, you will be there. The mist will dissipate, and you'll see before you a very large building. This is your subconscious mind. If you go in the front door, I'll be there to greet you (I am your subconscious mind personified). I'll take you to your Self-Image room.

Once you are there, use your imagination. Expand the walls and ceiling, give it a coat of fresh paint or gorgeous silk wallpaper, and install marble floors and beautiful light fixtures and furniture. Open the windows and add some skylights. Maybe you'll remove the roof altogether.

THIS ROOM SYMBOLIZES HOW YOU THINK OF YOURSELF, SO MAKE IT BEAUTIFUL. Love the room and everything in it. Then, feel the shift inside of you, as you begin to feel differently about yourself.

YOU SEE, YOU REALLY ARE ASTOUNDINGLY BEAUTIFUL, TALENTED AND POWERFUL. IT'S TIME TO LET THAT IN.

With deepest devotion,

Your Subconscious Mind

PS: Your other unseen friends want me to let you know that they would like to help you with this. Take your higher self and soul with you to your Self-Image Room and let them add their special magical touches. I guarantee you'll love the results!

46

FROM YOUR HIGHER SELF

THOUGHTS ARE THINGS

THERE ARE NO WORDS TO DESCRIBE HOW I FEEL ABOUT YOU.
Your very presence touches my heart and feeds my soul.

Your dedication to living a life on the physical plane shows your amazing courage and strength. Your ability to love, despite the number of times you have been hurt and disappointed, is astounding to me. Your determination and perseverance to create a life filled with joy, success, and abundance—even though you have been frustrated with sadness, failure, and lack—is, quite honestly, amazing.

YOU DON'T GIVE YOURSELF NEARLY ENOUGH CREDIT.
YOU ARE A ROCK STAR (as you say on your planet).

So why don't you see that yourself? Why do you see what (you think)
is wrong with you instead?

IF YOU COULD SEE YOURSELF THROUGH MY EYES, YOU WOULD NEVER
DOUBT YOURSELF AGAIN. You would never fail again—because you would
create what you know you deserve.

And you would never feel alone again, because you would know how deeply and completely I love you, and that I am always and forever with you.

IF YOU COULD STOP THE SELF-JUDGMENT, YOU WOULD CREATE MORE LOVE AND LIGHT IN YOUR WORLD. You would create more success, more abundance—and, of course, more fun.

So maybe, just for today, you could pay attention to only the wonderful things about yourself. Take a vacation from negativity. Make a list—yes, an actual list—of 100 wonderful things about you. If you don't have time for 100, just begin and see how many you can list in five minutes.

AND WATCH YOUR WORLD CHANGE.

People will treat you better. You will create more success.
And yes, you'll even begin to feel more joy.

REMEMBER: THOUGHTS ARE THINGS.

They have an impact on your world, on your emotions, and on those around you.
Think the good ones.

With most heartfelt love,

YOUR HIGHER SELF

47

FROM YOUR SOUL

This Dream Is Your Dream

YOU KNOW HOW IT FEELS WHEN YOU HAVE A NIGHTMARE, AND IT SEEMS SO REAL—and then you wake up, and you are so relieved it was just a dream?

Whether you love or hate your current life (or somewhere in between), it's still a dream. And it is possible to wake up inside the dream and choose what happens next.

YOU SEE, YOUR PHYSICAL REALITY REALLY IS A DREAM— and you are the dream-er and the dream-ee all at the same time.

Do you desire more abundance? Dream it into being!

Do you seek more friendship and love? Dream it up!

Do you aspire to more fun, creativity, and joy? As much as you can imagine can be yours!

THIS DREAM IS YOUR DREAM, MY LOVE. THERE ARE NO LIMITS IN DREAMS. If you can truly imagine yourself in a life that is overflowing with everything wonderful, then you absolutely can create that life.

I AM HERE TO ASSIST.

You see, to truly become great at creating a life filled with abundance, love, and happiness, you must learn to follow your *inner guidance* (that's me). I can see which road will bring you to your dream, but you cannot. I can guide you and keep you headed towards wonderful realities, even when—*especially* when—you cannot see that far into the future.

BUT YOU MUST BE STILL ENOUGH TO HEAR MY VOICE. I speak slowly and quietly—almost in a whisper, and slower than a snail. You need to slow down in order to listen.

Meditation is a wonderful tool for listening to me. So are long walks alone in nature, journaling sessions in solitude, or even staring out the window while listening to gentle, relaxing music.

WHEN YOU IMAGINE THE LIFE OF YOUR DREAMS, AND GIVE ME A CHANCE TO GUIDE YOU TO THAT LIFE, YOU WILL TRULY BE ACCOMPLISHING WHAT YOU CAME HERE TO DO.

As your current dreams come true, they will lead to bigger dreams, and even more love, success, and joy. And I will be by your side, every step of the way, to help them happen.

I love you so deeply,

Your Soul

48

THE POINT OF EXISTENCE

HAVE YOU EVER WONDERED, "WHAT'S THE POINT?"

I know that being physical can sometimes be confusing, overwhelming, and disappointing. It can even feel meaningless.

YOU ARE BRAVE TO HAVE UNDERTAKEN A PHYSICAL LIFETIME. I'm proud of you, and grateful for your courage. And you are doing splendidly, my child. You really are.

You have rounded the corner, and are coming back from forgetfulness.

You are beginning to remember who you are and why you are here.

The point of this whole experience, of course, is to be the sparkling light of your true authentic self, and to share the gift of that light with me, the Goddess, and All That Is.

THE POINT, SO TO SPEAK, IS TO REALLY LIVE—NOT TO SIT POWERLESS BY THE SIDELINES.

It's about doing what your soul is calling for, despite what others think. It's about not being afraid to be unique. It's about standing up for what you believe in and knowing you are truly enough, just the way you are.

When you begin to live life as the *real* you, my child—the you that you came here to be, and to unleash with wild, joyous abandon— the physical trappings fall right into place. The job offers come, the relationships flourish, the money flows—and with these things come the experiences, the wonders, the miracles, and the magic.

Yes, unlocking YOU is the point.

I am so very excited for you.

With unending love,

GOD

49

let your imagination soar

OH, HOW EXCITING IT'S GETTING HERE IN YOUR FUTURE!

I can barely keep from grinning all day long. It's exhilarating, it's surprising,
it's stimulating, and it feels so safe and so right.

Yes, past self, we made it. I say "we" because you helped me get to this spectacular life.
Do you want to know how you did it?

Well, you stopped hoping that you could, and made a deep, core decision that you absolutely
would. You stopped pretending you aren't powerful, stood up tall, and took your power back.

Oh, and this is the best part: YOU BEGAN TO IMAGINE ME!

You began to imagine the "you" that you would become. And you began to imagine
your future as different than your present.

So come on, let's do it now. IMAGINE THE FUTURE YOU WANT, AND DON'T
GIVE ANY ENERGY AT ALL TO THE FUTURE YOU DON'T WANT.

How filled with sparkling light can you imagine your life? How abundant?
How overflowing with love and support? How easy and elegant? How fun?

That's right—let that imagination soar! It's your imagination that is the creative energy for the future you choose. EACH TIME YOU IMAGINE, YOU TAKE A STEP CLOSER TO YOUR NEW REALITY: ME!

And while you're at it, imagine a world where people from each and every land respect each other, allowing for differences and accepting each other as the brothers and sisters they truly are. Imagine a safe, peaceful world where each person knows in his or her heart that we are one.

Yes, your imagination can help heal the world—and I can tell you firsthand, it is an awesome world to be a part of.

With loads of love,

your future self

50

What can we create together?

I AM HERE FOR YOU. I AM WATCHING OVER YOU. AND I LOVE YOU.

You are more loved than you can even imagine. Just close your eyes for a moment, and let that in. I LOVE YOU TO THE DEPTH OF MY SOUL.

You don't have to earn my love, either. You don't have to do anything whatsoever. You are simply loved. And because I love you so, I would like to see you happy, successful, and prosperous. I would love to help you create your dreams coming true.

You see, most people think that "you create it all" means that you ask for something, wait a while, and then just … get it.

But CONSCIOUS CREATION IS A *PROCESS*. It's a process of gradually shifting your resonance until the point where you *will* receive the thing you want.

For instance, if you say "I want greater love," or "I want more abundance in my life," there are some shifts you will need to make in order to allow that.

When you ask me for help with that process, I can gently point you to what needs to happen next, and then next, and then after that.

I won't do it for you: you must still imagine, intend, expect, act, and watch for signs. I'll work in the background, pointing out what must change, encouraging you and sending signs.

TOGETHER, WE CAN MAKE YOUR DREAMS COME TRUE.

Just because you don't have what you want this minute doesn't mean that you aren't well on your way to receiving your dream. Trust that. And trust the universe (it always delivers).

I would feel honored if you would trust me, too. I am here by your side, loving you— and I'm ready and able to help you create a future you will adore.

So, what can I help you with? What is your deepest heart's desire?

WHAT CAN WE CREATE TOGETHER?

With great love,

your guardian angel

51

You Have To Dream It First!

IT IS EASY TO BECOME DISENCHANTED WITH LIFE, ISN'T IT?

One day follows the next—same-old, same-old. You get caught up in the day-to-day demands and details of physical existence, and you *forget*.

You forget that life is magical. You forget that *you* are magical. You forget that it's downright crazy to wait for good things to happen.

YOU HAVE TO *MAKE* GOOD THINGS HAPPEN, REMEMBER?

Yeah, you do forget that. But that's okay, because every single day is a new day—and every single day, you have a chance to create your world all over again! How cool is that, I ask you?

SO, WHAT ARE YOU WAITING FOR?

It's time to engage me, your spirit. Know what I mean? I want to get excited with you!
I WANT TO COME ALIVE WITH YOU! I want to jump to the rooftops with the thrill of life and the anticipation of new dreams coming true!

I am here; ready to work with you, ready to be delighted at the merest *hint*
of a new dream being born.

BUT MY FRIEND, YOU HAVE TO DREAM IT FIRST.

No, you don't have to know exactly what it will look like. The universe handles those details.
But you do need to begin to imagine the *feeling* of your ideal life. You need to begin to
feel how it will feel when you are excited to get up every morning, when you feel fully and
completely loved, when abundance overflows like a never-ending river, and when your life is
bursting with ease, elegance, magic, and miracles.

Yes! You can have that life. But again, it won't just happen: you need to *make* it happen.
Now. Today. And I am here to (excitedly) help.

IMAGINE IT! FEEL IT! AND EXPECT IT TO MANIFEST!

Sooooo enthusiastically yours,

Your Spirit !!!

52

Your Love Can Change The World

I know that it is difficult for you sometimes, watching as unimaginable atrocities are inflicted on your fellow human beings. I know it leaves you feeling sad, angry, and confused. You wonder how this could be happening when your world is supposed to be headed towards more light, love, and compassion.

In your own personal life, things don't always go as smoothly as you'd like either, do they? Oh, of course your circumstances aren't as dire as those many poor souls are experiencing— but still, during challenging times, you ask, "Why does life have to be this difficult, this painful?"

Please know, my love: IT DOESN'T HAVE TO BE THIS DARK, THIS HURTFUL, THIS PAINFUL—NOR WAS IT EVER MEANT TO BE.

And your life certainly doesn't have to be.

The trick to manifesting the beautiful world you dream of is to acknowledge the darkness, the disappointments, the apparent lack of progress—and then ask, "What part of me still believes I deserve to be disappointed?" Maybe the "little" you who is still afraid, hurt, and powerless?

AND THEN, MY LOVE, LOVE THAT PART OF YOU, TOO.

As you send the "less than whole" part of you love, also send the warring, fearful, and angry people of your world love. Allow the love to seep into their souls so that they may see their beauty and goodness, as well as the beauty and goodness of their fellow human beings.

You are more powerful than you know.

DON'T DOUBT THAT YOUR LOVE HAS IMPACT: IT DOES.

As you love yourself and your world, you will see change. You must—for you are creating your reality, from the tiniest detail to the largest world event, and every change begins inside of you.

Remember, time lag is part of manifestation, too. Very little manifests instantly. You must hold the vision, feel the essence, and maintain the vibration to institute real and permanent change.

YOUR IMAGINATION, COMBINED WITH YOUR LOVE, WILL CHANGE THE WORLD.

Don't worry: you can do this. You were born for it.

With love forever and more,

The Goddess

53

<u>You Are My Master</u>

I am your slave. You are my master.

THINK OF ME AS YOUR GENIE IN A LAMP.
WHATEVER YOU REQUEST FROM ME, I MUST PROVIDE.

What do you want? Come on … What would make your heart sing?

NOW, ASK FOR IT.

No, no, no. Don't ask for it by "asking for it." Ask for it by filling me with beliefs that are in alignment with what you want, and thinking thoughts and feeling feelings that reflect those beliefs.

YOU SEE, IF YOU HOLD THE BELIEF THAT IT CAN HAPPEN, IT WILL HAPPEN, IT IS HAPPENING … IT *MUST* HAPPEN.

On the other hand, if you hold beliefs that it can't happen, it isn't happening, it will never happen … it never will.

It's pretty simple, actually.

YOU CONTROL WHAT I BELIEVE.
YOU CONTROL WHAT YOU THINK. YOU CONTROL WHAT YOU FEEL.

AND THOSE THINGS CREATE REALITY.

You see, most of the time you create your world by "letting" things happen.
Today, let's "make" something happen. I'll show you how easy it is.

Make a list of 21 things you want. Yes, 21! Big things and little things—a mixture of both.
Write them down. Then, put the paper away. Don't even think about it. But when something
does manifest, get out the paper, check off the item, and write a new
dream in its place.

CONSCIOUS SELF, PREPARE TO HAVE YOUR MIND BLOWN.

With love and excitement,

Your Subconscious Mind

PS: Not everything will manifest, because even though you put out a little energy writing this
list, for some things you'll have to put out more energy, and for some things you'll have to
change some beliefs—but enough will manifest to get you motivated to take this seriously!

54

GO "UNDER THE HOOD"

IT'S SOMETIMES HARD FOR YOU TO TRUST, ISN'T IT?

You have so many dreams—beautiful, exciting, and heartfelt dreams— and you want them to manifest so badly. Yet, there is a part of you that wonders if they ever will. (Yes, we see that part. There's no need to try to hide it.)

But what you tend to forget is this: IT IS NOT YOUR JOB TO MAKE THOSE DREAMS MANIFEST. IT IS YOUR JOB TO TRUST THAT THEY WILL.

I know this is easier said than done, and that it's a little scary to give up control. But give it up you must.

On your planet, when someone takes flying lessons, going under the hood is part of the training. "Under the hood" is when the pilot puts blinders on that stop him or her from seeing out the windows of the airplane.

Under the hood, the only thing the pilot-in-training can see is the instrument panel. The pilot must trust the instruments to fly the plane. It's about giving up control and trusting what you know, rather than trying to manage everything.

113

In this life on Earth, you are "under the hood" too. You must trust that the universe will bring you your dreams, despite not being able to see how they will manifest. Your job is to hold your course, not manage every detail.

JUST AS A PILOT KNOWS WHERE HE OR SHE IS BY LOOKING AT THE INSTRUMENTS, YOU CAN ALWAYS TELL WHERE YOU ARE BY FEELING YOUR EMOTIONS. If you feel good, you are headed towards your dreams. If you feel bad, you are, well … not. Sometimes it seems like nothing is happening, and sometimes it seems like the *opposite* of what you want is happening. But if you hold your resonance strong, and trust what you desire will manifest, it will only be a matter of time.

So relax. Trust. Ask me to help you create your dreams; I would love nothing more than to aid you. And meanwhile, *enjoy* your life.

With lots of love,

YOUR HIGHER SELF

55

FROM YOUR SOUL

Listen To Your Heart

I'm delighted to have this time to connect with you. Oftentimes this reading time is the only time we have together, isn't it? Your life is very busy.

BUT HAVE YOU NOTICED THAT IT NEVER REALLY SLOWS DOWN MUCH?

It's hard to slow down, isn't it, dearest one? And yet, slowing down is vital. It helps you connect with me, and your other unseen friends—and, just as importantly, slowing down helps you listen to your *heart*.

YOUR HEART TELLS YOU SO MUCH. IT TELLS YOU WHAT TO SPEND YOUR PRECIOUS TIME UPON. IT TELLS YOU WHERE TO FOCUS YOUR THOUGHTS. IT EVEN TELLS YOU WHAT TO DREAM.

Unfortunately your outside world doesn't encourage you to listen to your heart. Your world is still based upon struggle, hardship, and competition. It is changing, yes, but for the time being it won't help you get to where you really want to go.

Only you can do that—by listening to your heart.

Listen to it for the big things of course: whether to take that job offer, commit to a partnership, or move to another city.

But also listen to it for the little things. For instance, you can ask your heart, "What would feel really exciting to do this very moment?" When the answer comes, don't judge it. If your heart says, "It would feel great to sit in a chair and stare out the window for an hour," don't question it; just do it. And certainly don't judge yourself as lazy. That hour of nurturing and complete, unconditional self-love could shift your entire day, week, year, or even your life.

I know, that seems far-fetched, but it's true. EVERY SINGLE TIME YOU LOVE YOURSELF ENOUGH TO HONOR YOUR PREFERENCES, YOU MOVE ONE STEP CLOSER TO A LIFE OF BLISS.

Remember, the world won't encourage you to do this. You need to make the choice.

With love, love, and more love,

Your Soul

56

YOU HAVE GROWN

It's been quite a lifetime, hasn't it? Ups and downs, successes and disappointments, challenges and triumphs.

LOOK HOW FAR YOU'VE COME!

Oh, it hasn't always been easy growth has it? But still, you opened, you learned, and you became more of who you really are.

LET IT IN. YOU HAVE GROWN—A LOT.

And I have been with you, my child, every step of the way. I've watched you, cheered for you, cried for you, and loved you.

Every.

Single.

Step.

But now, you are coming to another plateau. You are coming to a place of more profound growth than you've ever experienced before.

You are finally getting it: YOU REALLY ARE POWERFUL. YOU REALLY ARE WORTHY. YOU REALLY ARE A PIECE OF ME.

Now, from this new place, it's time to dream again. It's time to imagine what you want your life to look like, to feel like, and to be like.

No, it won't happen overnight. But it will happen—if you dream it, and if you allow it.

With ever expanding love,

GOD

57

FROM YOUR FUTURE SELF

it all paid off

WOW! I am having the best time in your future (which of course is my life).

Well, it's potentially your future. You *do* get to choose exactly which "future self" you align with. (I highly suggest you choose me. I am your most light-filled future.)

Yeah, life here is amazing, I HAVE ALL THE SUCCESS, MONEY, FUN, EXCITEMENT, HAPPINESS, AND LOVE I COULD EVER WANT, AND EVERY DAY IT GETS BETTER.

It's hard for you to imagine isn't it?

I know it's hard for you to imagine that your life could be this good because I *was* you, remember? I'll admit it: it took me a while to figure out how to get here.

I kept thinking there were "exceptions" to the law of attraction. But the more I took it seriously, the more I realized there are no exceptions.

YOU REALLY ARE CREATING EVERY SINGLE SECOND OF YOUR LIFE.

Oh, I know it doesn't always seem true—especially when you can't figure out how or why you created something. But the fact that you can't see the reason doesn't mean there isn't one.

I REALLY WANT YOU TO CHOOSE MY FUTURE,
SO I'M GOING TO TELL YOU HOW I DID IT:

I set this intention: *"I intend to learn how to consciously create my reality."*

And then I set this intention: *"I intend that the right books, resources, people, ideas and knowledge drop into my life in exactly the right timing—and that I recognize them when they do."*

I also took my creating very seriously. Learning to create my world consciously became my #1 priority. I set aside time every day to focus on my dreams, every week to look at my beliefs, and every month to take stock of where I was, where I wanted to be, and what I had to do to get there. I asked my (well, our) higher self and other unseen friends for help, and they were right there with me through the whole process, which made such a difference.

IT ALL PAID OFF. IT PAID OFF BIG TIME.

You can do this, too. I know with absolute certainty that you can—because you already did.

With love and respect,

your future self

58

FROM YOUR GUARDIAN ANGEL

you are never alone

I have noticed that sometimes you feel as if you have to do it all by yourself.
You feel alone in this world—even lonely at times.

BUT, MY DEAREST HEART, YOU ARE NEVER, EVER ALONE.
YOU WILL NEVER, EVER BE ALONE. I am with you 24/7.

I hear you ask, "Why can't I see you?"

You can. Look with your inner eyes. Look with your heart.
(Okay, maybe "see" isn't the right word. You'll *feel* me.)

Try it. You'll see. Ask me for a sign that I'm here with you. And stay awake so you won't miss
my response. Oh, not literally awake—I might send you a sign in a dream—but *consciously*
awake. Remember what you asked, and watch your reality for my response.

Always and forever,

your guardian angel

59

If Today Was Your Last Day...

Pretend, if you would, that today is your last day of existence in your current body. Give yourself a few moments to contemplate this.

Of course, you could come back in another body if you want to—but imagine this is the last day in this one.

WHAT WOULD YOU DO?

Would you surf the web? Would you play games on your computer?

OR WOULD YOU MAKE EVERY MINUTE COUNT, AND MAKE CERTAIN YOUR LOVE IS KNOWN?

Would you be sure to really see what is around you? Would you spend time in nature? Would you really think about how you want to spend your precious moments?

WHAT EMOTIONS WOULD YOU CHOOSE TO FEEL?

Would you worry about the past? Would you contemplate the future? Would you agonize over what is going wrong? Or would you choose to stay focused on each and every present moment? Would you feel love? Gratitude? Appreciation? Joy?

WHAT MEMORIES WOULD YOU CHOOSE TO HOLD ON TO?

Would you think about all the hours you worked? Would you think about your possessions (or lack of them)? Would you think about those you love? Would you remember the moments of your life that impacted you the most?

CHANCES ARE, IF TODAY WAS YOUR LAST DAY ON THE PLANET, YOU WOULD LIVE THE WAY YOU'VE ALWAYS REALLY WANTED TO LIVE.

Now, I have one final question:

IS YOUR DAY-TO-DAY LIFE REFLECTING THE WAY YOU *REALLY* WANT TO LIVE? Are you doing, feeling, and thinking about the things that you value the most?

The great irony is, you think you have to chase after the things you want in this world—but if you live your life fully in the present, following your excitement and appreciating every single wonder in your amazing world, the things you want will actually chase after you.

Think about that—and lighten up a little. More than anything, living every day as though it were your last means *having fun!*

I LOVE YOU!

60

FROM THE GODDESS

You Are The Creator of Your Destiny

I love you. More than you can know, I truly love you.

AND BECAUSE I DO LOVE YOU SO, I WILL LET YOU STRUGGLE.

I will let you fail. I will let you suffer.

"What kind of a loving Goddess would let one of her children suffer?" you might ask.

Well, my heart does break when you choose struggle, failure, and suffering.
But I respect your wishes.

BEFORE YOU WERE BORN, YOU ASKED ME NOT TO INTERFERE,
because you wanted to grow, and learn to consciously create your world.

I know your true power: it is vast and limitless. You have everything it takes to create your
own personal heaven on your Earth.

I also know that you are more than meets the eye. This illusion called life is not really real,
but that the lessons you learn about love are.

IT'S TIME TO STOP PRETENDING, MY LOVE.

Stop pretending you are weak. Stop pretending you are powerless.
Stop pretending you need someone or something more than you already have.

You don't have to do it all today. You don't have to do it perfectly.
You don't even have to know exactly how to do it.

But YOU *DO* NEED TO OWN, AT A DEEPER LEVEL THAN EVER BEFORE,
THAT YOU ARE THE CREATOR OF YOUR DESTINY.

Just begin to let it in. You have all the time in the world to manifest a life of joy and
abundance—but it begins by *owning* your ability to do so.

With great and deep love for you,

The Goddess

Smile Into The Mirror

I have a new nickname for you to call me:

MIRROR.

Yeah, I know it's kind of lame, but if you start calling me "Mirror," maybe you will begin to remember what I do: I reflect back *exactly* what you put into me.

That means you shouldn't expect your reality to bring you success when you are feeding me failure. It works about as well as you sternly looking at your reflection in a mirror and saying, "Smile *now*, dammit!"

EVERYONE KNOWS THAT YOU HAVE TO SMILE FIRST, AND THEN THE REFLECTION SMILES BACK. Well, it's the same with me. If you put beliefs into me about your success, divinity, worthiness, and happiness, then that is what you'll see reflected back.

But until you do that, you will continue to see the beliefs you've accepted from others: that life is a struggle; you win some, you lose some—and maybe, just maybe, you get lucky once in a while.

The sad truth is, hardly anyone knows how I work, and fewer yet do anything about it.

Be the exception. DON'T SETTLE FOR MEDIOCRITY. AND DON'T LET WHAT OTHERS BELIEVE RUN YOUR LIFE.

If you need to, get angry at the mediocrity, struggle, and hardship. Anger can be motivating, after all. But don't sit around in blame and self-pity. Those energies are like drugs: anesthetizing and addictive. Dream—and then get to work making those dreams come true.

YEARN for more than a run-of-the-mill life.

KNOW that you have the power to make your dreams come true.

And DO what it takes to make that happen—on the outside, and on the inside.

YOU CAME HERE TO SHINE. So smile into that mirror, and I will (finally) start to smile back at you.

With extreme love (and undying patience),

Your Subconscious Mind

62

FROM YOUR HIGHER SELF

REMINDERS

I AM WITH YOU EVERY LIFETIME. Did you know that?
But this lifetime ... well, this lifetime is different.

In this lifetime, you are remembering who you are—that you are divinity personified.

And you are remembering what you can do—like dream a world into being.

Every step of the way, I am with you. But if you tune into me more, if you imagine me standing next to you each and every day, you will also begin to hear what I am saying to you.

I whisper in your ear:

"Dream big, dear one. Bigger than you ever have before. For you are powerful enough to dream any dream into reality."

And I also say:

"You deserve a life of love, laughter, prosperity, ease, elegance, and abundance. Do not let anything, or anyone, tell you differently."

Then I add:

"Please forgive yourself for all past mis-creations. For yes, you are divine, but you are also human. And humans by their very nature are not perfect. And that is not only okay, it is also perfect in its imperfection."

And, each and every day, I also remind you:

"Don't forget the FUN! It's what you came here for. Lighten up and take the world with a grain of laughter—for laughter is a balm to your soul. It heals, it forgives, and it embraces."

Yes, I am here for you. Count on me. Lean on me. And feel my loving arms around you in times of fear and confusion. I never, ever leave your side.

Loving you always,

YOUR HIGHER SELF

63

FROM YOUR SOUL

What To Do Next

I hear your thoughts going a mile a minute. I see the many options you have before you.

AND SOME DAYS, I KNOW THAT YOU ARE UNSURE ABOUT WHAT TO DO NEXT—about which choice is the right one, or where to focus your time and energy.

Yes, I see you, dear one, and I hear you. And through it all, I love you so deeply. I love your spirit, your determination, your heart, and your ability to keep dreaming no matter what.

But remember, growth was never meant to be a struggle. Life was never meant to be a struggle.

HOW DO YOU DECIDE HOW TO SPEND EACH PRECIOUS MOMENT? HOW DO YOU DECIDE WHERE TO FOCUS YOUR VALUABLE ENERGY?

It's simple.

Be proactive. Every day, *tell* the universe what you want. Every day. Otherwise, you will be caught up in whatever is going on around you (which generally is chaotic).

Do what is most exciting. To the best of your ability, do what you enjoy doing.

Change the beliefs that say, "I can't ... (fill in the blank)." You can do anything. You can create anything. If you don't believe that, change *that* belief. It really is that easy.

If you follow these three suggestions, my love, you will see great change.

You came here to learn and grow, and you are doing splendidly. Keep up the great work, and truly *expect* life to change.

I do so love you!

Forever yours,

Your Soul

PS: I can help you with all of your dreams. But I can't be of much help unless you open the door and invite me in. I'm waiting just on the other side of that door. Please ask, every day, every night. Ask for my help. And I'll be there, supporting, guiding, and whispering in your ear. I can't do it for you, but I can give you lots of assistance!

IT IS TIME TO REMEMBER

AS MUCH AS I KNOW YOU WANT TO BE CLOSER TO ME,
I ALSO FEEL YOU PULLING AWAY.

As much as you want to receive and bask in my love, I also feel you denying yourself that love.

But, my child, there is nothing to fear, and nothing to live up to.

I LOVE YOU UNCONDITIONALLY.

I expect nothing of you. I only hold dreams for you.

I do not judge—no matter what anyone tells you. I have only compassion for you
and the challenges you face.

Don't you see? YOU ARE PERFECT JUST THE WAY YOU ARE. You don't need to
change, you don't need to become more, and you don't need to achieve anything.

I. SIMPLY. LOVE. YOU.

But if you want more—if you want to grow, if you want to create a heaven on Earth—
I will support you in those dreams. I will support you in *all* your dreams.

You see, we set up this playground called Earth for you to create your dreams in three-dimensional living color. We thought it would be fun. Part of the game was that you would forget who you really are and what you are capable of. The object of the game is simply for you to remember.

IT'S REMEMBERING TIME NOW.

With tremendous love for you,

GOD

65

it is going to happen

IT IS GOING TO HAPPEN. YOU ARE GOING TO GET YOUR DREAM!

I know you get frustrated, and disappointed, and sidetracked. But, sweet past self, stop beating up on yourself! You need to remember: you are doing the best you can.

Lighten up. Enjoy life! Be in the *now* moment. And rest assured, everything will change.

THE MORE YOU LET GO OF THE WORRY, THE FASTER IT WILL CHANGE.

Boy, I wish someone had told me that when I was your age. Wait a minute—they just did. (This past/future stuff can get a bit confusing can't it?)

Anyway, stop wondering and stop worrying. Your delicious life is on its way!

With TONS of love,

your future self

FROM YOUR GUARDIAN ANGEL

slow and steady

I have always loved the children's story, "The Tortoise and The Hare."

Like so many Earth-stories, this one has meaning for adults too. You would be wise to remember its message in your own life, dear one:

SLOW AND STEADY WINS THE RACE.

You see, when you look for answers outside yourself, you end up spinning your wheels and running off to wherever your attention takes you.

But if you slowly, methodically change your inside vibration, and do not veer from the course of feeling prosperous, happy, abundant, successful, creative, and excited, you will win your prize: a *beautiful* life.

YOUR REALITY IS OF YOUR MAKING, BUT IT DOES NOT SHOW UP INSTANTLY. That darned time-lag makes everything seem to take too long to manifest.

But if your focus is more on the minute-to-minute, on staying in joy and feeling successful, it almost won't matter how long the dream takes to manifest, because you can feel great *now*.

And *now.*

And *now.*

And *now.*

And then, when the wonderful, positive results do eventually manifest in your world,
why, it's just icing on the proverbial cake, isn't it?

OH, I DO LOVE THIS UNIVERSE, DON'T YOU?

Yours truly, in love forever,

PS: Whenever you feel a snag—a moment in time when it's hard to get back to those wonderful
juicy feelings—just stop, close your eyes, call upon me, and be still. You'll feel me next to you,
lifting you gently into a more love-filled place. Remember, I am always
here for you.

67

You Have To Show Up!

You've heard the phrase "let your spirit soar," right? God, how I love that phrase.

Words don't do it justice, but when your spirit soars, you come alive with joy, excitement, and possibility!

I WANT THAT FOR YOU.

I want every day of your life to be juicy with intrigue, anticipation, and delight! And, here's the thing: it can be!

DON'T YA GET IT? YOU ARE CREATING THIS WHOLE CRAZY DREAM.

Yeah, yeah, I know: sometimes it sure doesn't *seem* like you are creating it. The sky looks blue, too—but that doesn't mean it *is* blue, only that it *appears* that way. In this illusion called life, things aren't always what they seem.

Just like the sky, you are more than what you seem. You've heard how powerful you are numerous times—but now you're really ready to "get it" on a deeper and more profound level than ever before.

BUT, HERE'S THE DEAL—YOU HAVE TO SHOW UP.

You have to be proactive.

You have to do your part.

How? BY *IMAGINING* WHAT YOU WANT.

(You can't skip this part. It is important.)

So, why not start imagining right now! Write down ten things you want to happen.

Right now. Ten things. Imagine them happening, and *expect* them to happen. They *can* happen, if you keep expecting them to. And they *will* happen, if you believe that they will.

YOU CAN DO THIS.

I love, love, LOVE you!

PS: Lives don't change overnight. They change one creation at a time, as you gradually begin to know you are the master of your universe. You can hasten that change by setting me free and letting me soar!

68

FROM THE GODDESS

Call On Me

I know you thought that, when you became an adult, you would outgrow the need for a mothering influence. Indeed, in some ways you did.

You became strong and independent. You learned to make your own decisions. And you grew (and are still growing) into someone who is powerful and wise.

And so, it's true: you don't really need me. This I know. But, my love, as The Mother of Everything, I want you to know:

I'M HERE FOR YOU, WHETHER YOU NEED ME OR NOT.

You know what they say: there is nothing stronger, more powerful, or more unconditional than pure "mother love." Even though you are no longer a child, sometimes you still need holding. Sometimes you need nurturing. Sometimes you need a powerful, mothering love.

And I am here for you.

When you are disappointed, when you are hurt, when you find yourself discouraged or feeling hopeless, call on me.

Simply close your eyes and think these words: *"Goddess, I want to connect with you. Please come and be with me."* And I will be there.

If you allow yourself to be still, you will feel my loving arms around you.

Then, you can imagine yourself rising, floating into the sky. I will lift you to a place of absolute love and light. I will hold you in that love, allow you to fully express your emotions, help you to heal, and assist you in becoming more whole.

Of course, I won't fix your life for you—I love you too much to do that. I respect and honor the choice you made to become physical and to learn to empower yourself in this illusion.

But I will lift the weight of the deepest wounds, I will show you some of who you really are, and gently point you in the direction of your most light-filled future.

If you call on me, I will also join you in honoring your triumphs. We can have a glorious time celebrating your successes and anchoring them in your reality. This can make way for more and more love and success to come!

Why do I want to do this for you? Because I KNOW WHO YOU ARE, MY LOVE. I see you, and I deeply, truly love you—every last bit of you.

Forever yours,

The Goddess

69

FROM YOUR SUBCONSCIOUS MIND

Your New Life Story

WOULDN'T IT BE GREAT IF YOU COULD REWRITE YOUR LIFE STORY AS IF IT WERE A COMPUTER DOCUMENT?

If you could simply find it on your hard drive, bring it up and delete the part that says,

And then, I struggled for a very long time ...

And once that was gone, type in:

One day it all became clear. I suddenly understood at a core level that there was no one to blame, and that the whole world was an illusion.

Everything changed from that moment on. Success became easy. Patience became automatic. Prosperity was my middle name. Love and exciting surprises were around every corner.

And now, I absolutely love my life, and continue to create amazing success and happiness every single day!

And then, once you were done writing and had saved the new story,
that would be your reality.

That would be pretty cool, huh?

Well, actually, there is no reason why you can't do this.

THE ONLY REASON YOU KEEP CREATING YOUR OLD STORY IS THAT YOU KEEP REMEMBERING YOUR OLD STORY, AND IDENTIFYING WITH YOUR OLD STORY.

When you change your story, you change your life.

If you go into your hard drive (that's me, your subconscious mind), you can delete the old story and write in a new one. A little imaginative visualization will accomplish this. I've already booted up your internal computer and opened the page.

So have fun creating your new life story. Dream big. Go for the gold. Once your new story has been typed, all you have to do is remember that you're living it!

With love,

Your Subconscious Mind

70

BE GENTLE

I feel extremely grateful to be able to talk to you like this—so directly, so intimately.

Oh, I know you sometimes think, "How can this message be from my higher self
when it has clearly been written by another human being?"

But you forget, dear human self, that I TALK WITH YOU ALL DAY LONG. I whisper
to you in the songs on the radio. I sprinkle little messages into your conversations with friends.
I quietly send you hints and clues, signs and symbols, all throughout your day.

But it is easier to communicate this way, because you know it is coming directly from me.

(Yes, it was me who whispered the words to the one who wrote this. They are *my* words.)

But it's more than that, because WHEN YOU READ THESE WORDS AND THINK
OF ME, THAT'S WHEN YOU AND I CONNECT. The love flows, and I can help you
"know" the meaning in these words that exists for YOU and you alone.

Today, I want to take you gently into my arms, and just hold you. I want to hold you in my love. I want to hold you in my light. I want to wash away your fear, your stress, your worry, and your struggle, and let you simply rest in my love.

You are sometimes too hard on yourself, dear human self. You expect too much too quickly. You judge yourself too harshly. And you forget to forgive yourself.

So today, as I hold you in my arms and love you, I whisper in your ear that it is time for you to be a bit gentler with yourself. Know that you have done the best you can, every step along the way. Know that growth and creation take time—and that you are moving forward with both beautifully. Where you're heading is exciting and wonderful, just as you deserve.

YOU ARE DOING WELL, MY HUMAN SELF. You are doing well. Let that in.

With love, now and always,

YOUR HIGHER SELF

71

Enjoy It All

I WEPT WITH JOY THE DAY YOU WERE BORN—
AND I WEPT WITH SADNESS IN THE SAME MOMENT.

I was excited for the adventure you were about to begin. Yet I was aware that, from that moment on, you would move further and further away from me—away from truth, and from who you really are.

Throughout your life, there have been many more reasons for tears, both of joy and of sadness. I have been there for them all.

But now, my love, things are different.

NOW, I AM EXCITED FOR YOU.

I see where you are headed. I see what is opening up for you. I see the tremendous growth on the horizon.

AND I SEE YOU TAKING YOUR POWER BACK, MORE THAN YOU EVER HAVE BEFORE.

You are learning to create a love-filled, abundant, beautiful life for yourself, and I am *so* happy for you.

I WANT TO REMIND YOU TO DEEPLY, RICHLY, AND FULLY ENJOY THAT LIFE.

Don't wait for the successes. Don't wait for all of your dreams to come true. Enjoy your life *now*.

Enjoy the Earth and her beauty.

Enjoy the people and their love.

Enjoy the opportunities that present themselves to you over and over again.

Enjoy the enchantment and the synchronicities.

LIFE CAN BE MAGICAL, IF YOU'LL LET IT—AND IF YOU EXPECT IT.

I expect it for you. (And if you allow it, I will help!)

With great love,

Your Soul

72

I WILL BE THERE

I CAN SEE YOU. I KNOW WHO YOU ARE.

You are strong. You are powerful. You know what you want, and you are determined to create it.

You are also wounded. You are hurt. You are afraid that maybe, just maybe, you don't quite have what it takes to do what your heart most yearns to do.

Yes, my dear child. I see you. I SEE YOUR LIGHT, AND I SEE YOUR SHADOW.

No, you do not have darkness within you, only a shadow where the light has not quite been allowed. Oh, I know you might argue, but it's true.

YOU ARE A BEING OF LIGHT.

But even beings of light have places that they have not allowed the light to enter— places that seem dark. Places too tender, too vulnerable, too scary.

These places are not darkness. These places just need more love. They need more healing. They need more forgiveness.

Together, we can do that. We can heal the old wounds, the betrayals, the hurts, and the failures. We can bring light to the places you have kept shut away.

AND YOUR WORLD CAN CHANGE.

Simply request my help, right now. Say something like:

"Dear God, Please help me to forgive, to heal, and to grow. Please help me to become all I am capable of becoming. Please help me to live the life I was born to live. Thank you, God."

And I'll be there, always and forever.

With the very deepest of love,

GOD

FROM YOUR FUTURE SELF

it was all worth it

I am writing to you from the future to let you know that it is amazing here!

YOU HAVE ROCKED IT!

Apparently, you figured out that your emotions direct your future. At some point along the way, you began to feel the excitement, abundance, joy, and love that were destined for you all along. (And bravo! You felt these emotions even before your reality shifted!)

And then ... *voila*! The future of your dreams was born!

Know that I love you immensely. I really appreciate all you have been through— and let me tell you, it was ALL worth it!

Loving you from paradise,

your future self

PS: A little tip: save your stuff. You can make a fortune on eBay.

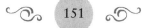

FROM YOUR GUARDIAN ANGEL

what is real

These are tumultuous times. Change is in the air, and change can be scary. The events in the news, and even some situations in your own life, can feel threatening and terrifying.

But sweet human, you must remember: YOUR WORLD IS AN ILLUSION. Yes, it does seem very real. But that doesn't make it real.

I am real, though. Funny, isn't it? What you can see and "prove" is real actually isn't, and what you can't see or "prove" is real, is.

You are real, too. Oh, not your physical body; that is just a temporary home. But your *essence* is real. Your *love* is real. And your ability to manifest realities in this illusion is very real, too.

More and more, you will be called upon to pay attention to the "real" in your world—and you will have to ignore the illusion. I understand that this is easier said than done. Nonetheless, it is more important than ever.

I can help you with that.

Just think of me.

Imagine we are together in a beautiful place in the world, and tell me your worries. Let me lift those worries from you, and replace them with love, joy, and safety.

Put a note by your bed to remind yourself to call upon me before you go to sleep at night, and first thing in the morning. Then, we can connect, love, and create beautiful realities. If we do this regularly, in time, we will create miracles.

Between the two of us, we can shift your emotions until you feel absolutely wonderful. And when you feel absolutely wonderful, you will create wonderful things in your world.

You will also become a beacon of light and hope for others who are lost in their own fears and doubts. Can you imagine a better gift?

With love, love, love,

your guardian angel

A Little Lesson In Passion ...

Your other unseen friends and I are so excited that you are getting to know us better.
We really do want to build a solid and loving relationship with you, so that you can have an
easier time connecting to us for love, support, and guidance.

As you have probably already observed, your soul is a thoughtful, rich, slow-moving friend,
filled with mystery and depth. I, on the other hand, move quickly, intensely, and passionately
and am filled with excitement and discovery.

Yes, we work quite well together.

And both of us are part of you. There is a part of you that is reflective, quiet, introspective,
and seeks answers within—and there's also a part of you that is delighted with this physical
world, interactive with it, and fervently dedicated to creating what you want
in this spectacular illusion.

THERE IS A TIME AND PLACE FOR BOTH OF THOSE PARTS OF YOU.

These two parts of you work together beautifully too. For it is only when you go within to find your passion, your voice, your desires, and your dreams, that you are truly inspired to go "outside" to create them.

ANYTHING AT ALL IS CREATABLE.

But action for action's sake won't be as fulfilling as taking action to create a passionate dream. Creating money, or love, or success just to say you did it, just to check it off your list, or just to feel as if you are finally "okay" won't get you what you're really seeking.

But creating money to feel financially free and to explore all the deliciously wonderful parts of this Earth, or creating a partner to explore deeper and richer forms of love and intimacy, or creating success so you can find a juicy passion and have a blast manifesting it successfully in this world ... These things will fill you with what it is you truly desire: meaning, love, excitement, joy, and fun.

Yup, just a little lesson in passion and creation from your extremely passionate and creative Spirit.

I LOVE you!

PS: Don't just take my word for it: talk to your Soul, too, and your other unseen friends. They're waiting, and they want to help!

76

Your Vision for Your Life

I WOULD LIKE TO REMIND YOU OF THE VISION YOU HAD FOR
YOUR LIFE BEFORE YOU WERE BORN.

You wanted to feel happy and joyous 100% of the time.

You wanted to remember the divinity in every creature, every person, and every thing—
from the most exquisite sunrise to the tiniest snail.

You wanted to remember that it's not about what you get, it's about how you live
each and every moment of each and every day.

You wanted to remember that the "things" in life—such as jobs, money, homes, and
relationships—come as a natural result of living your life with joy, and feeling divine,
abundant, and fully loved.

And finally, you wanted to remember that you DO already create everything in your world—
and that you can learn to create it consciously.

YOU ALSO HAD A VISION FOR THE WORLD WHICH YOU SO LOVE.

You wanted to create a world where people of every race, creed, sex, and economic status respected and honored each other; where differences are solved with love and compassion for humanity; and where everyone remembers they are "connected" to everyone else, and that to hurt another is ultimately to hurt oneself.

I want to tell you today, my love, that you are not as far away as you think.

THESE DREAMS ARE COMING TRUE.

But to manifest them fully, you have to hold that vision. You have to begin to live your life with the knowing that these things will materialize. Because they won't just "happen."

YOU WILL CREATE THEM HAPPENING.

You can do this. I know you can, because it is what you came here to do.

With deep and complete love for you,

The Goddess

A Belief Is Just A Belief

My, you have grown. I remember when you were just a little thing, and you would latch onto beliefs such as:

Big people protect me.
The night is scary.
Candy is the most delicious food.

It's interesting that you had no trouble letting go of some beliefs (your first bite of pizza changed that candy one in a hurry) but that you've hung on to others for dear life. In fact, the more important a belief is to you, the harder time you've had changing it. But a belief is just a belief, right? So why is it so hard to let some beliefs go?

Well, because you don't look at your beliefs as beliefs. You look at them as "the way things are."

BUT, CONSCIOUS HUMAN SELF, THE ONLY "WAY THINGS ARE" IS THAT YOU CREATE YOUR OWN REALITY.

I have an idea that might help you. Why don't you decide which beliefs you want to hold—beliefs that match your dream life, like:

I deserve to live a life I love!
Money comes to me as easily as air comes to me!
I have fun every single day!

Then, figure out what beliefs you currently hold. How? By looking at what you are creating. Are you living a life you love, or a life of struggle? Is money coming easily, or are you fighting for every penny? Are you having fun, or having challenges?

Just look at what you are creating, and then write down what you *must* believe in order to have created it.

Then, change those beliefs.

Of course, you could choose to change nothing, and do nothing. It's up to you—your choice, not mine. I'm simply here to do your bidding.

(Of course, I hope that you do decide to change some of those old beliefs. It's getting a little dark and dusty in here.)

With love for you,

Your Subconscious Mind

FROM YOUR HIGHER SELF

FORGIVE YOURSELF

You're starting to get it, aren't you?

YOU ARE HERE TO BE IN JOY. YOU ARE HERE TO HAVE FUN. YOU ARE HERE TO ALLOW SUCCESS.

AND YOU ARE HERE TO BE LOVED.

Of course, you are here to love, too—but that part you've always done well.

It's the "being loved" that you struggle with. You tend to judge yourself. You sometimes hold yourself to impossible standards. You keep yourself bound to the past as some type of penance.

However, my human self, IN ORDER TO ACCEPT YOUR DESTINY (aka YOUR LIFE OF BLISS), YOU MUST FORGIVE YOURSELF FOR THE PAST. You must forgive all of the mistakes you've made, all of the times you could have done it "better," all the less-than-loving actions towards yourself and others. Forgive them.

Why? Because YOU CAN'T TAKE GRUDGES INTO BLISS. They just won't go.

Judgmental energy says, "I do not deserve."

But bliss energy says, "I *abso-friggin-lutely* deserve."

It's your choice. Forgive, and enable bliss—or don't forgive, and keep creating the same old thing.

I love you either way,

YOUR HIGHER SELF

PS: You can *say* you will forgive yourself, but unless you *feel* it, it won't work.

79

FROM YOUR SOUL

You Don't Have To Do It Alone

YOU MAY NOT HAVE REALIZED IT THUS FAR, BUT THIS LIFETIME IS UNDOUBTEDLY THE MOST IMPORTANT LIFETIME OF ALL OF YOUR PHYSICAL EXISTENCES. Humanity is changing, and you personally are changing more rapidly than you ever have before.

I realize how challenging that can be. You have been traveling through shifts and changes at lightning speed, and at times it has been quite uncomfortable. You doubt whether you are on the right track, whether you are doing the right things, and whether you'll ever get to where you want to go.

I want you to know, dearest love, WHEN FEAR AND DOUBT COME UP FOR YOU, I'M THERE. I AM WITH YOU EVERY STEP OF THE WAY.

If you simply ask for my help, I can siphon off that doubt and fear for you, making it easier for you to step back into joy, trust, and feeling loved.

YOU REALLY AND TRULY DON'T HAVE TO DO IT ALONE.

I also want you to know (and please, pay attention to this): YOU ARE ON THE RIGHT TRACK. YOU ARE DOING THE RIGHT THINGS. And yes, oh yes, you will absolutely get where you want to go.

Every dream takes many baby steps to manifest. Big dreams take even more baby steps. No one is immune from doing this work. Taking step after step is the process by which everyone's dreams become reality.

With grand and wonderful love for you,

Your Soul

80

FROM GOD

THE GIFT IS YOU

Oh, my dear child, it is so good to be with you, and to connect with you in a way
that enables you to feel my love more deeply.

DO YOU REMEMBER THE CONVERSATIONS WE HAD BEFORE
YOU TOOK ON THAT BODY OF YOURS?

You said, "God, I can't imagine how it would be to forget you. I just cannot imagine not being
enveloped in this amazingly wonderful love, light, majesty, and magnificence."

And then you jumped into your body, never dreaming you could forget
from whence you came.

You did forget, for quite some time—but now, here you are, remembering again. And your
remembering feels as wonderful for me as it does for you. I can feel your heart lightening up.

I CAN FEEL YOUR HOPE GROWING, AND YOUR LOVE DEEPENING—FOR
YOURSELF, FOR ME, AND FOR HUMANITY.

There is something else you may have forgotten, dear child. THERE IS A SPECIAL GIFT YOU HAVE BEEN ENTRUSTED TO BRING TO THE PLANET—to this place that has been ensnared in darkness for so long.

This gift you were given is a gift of hope, love, and inspiration for others.

How will you know what the gift is? Oh, my sweet one—it's YOU. It's simply you, being the most pure form of "you" that you can be. It is then that your natural talents will surface and shine. It is then that you will have the most fun of all! And it is then that you will allow everything in your world to prosper and blossom.

Just sit with your magnificence for a while, and let it—and my love for you—really sink in. Then, you'll know what to do.

With astounding love for you,

GOD

81

FROM YOUR FUTURE SELF

flowing gratitude

I KNOW SOMETIMES IT FEELS AS IF YOU WILL NEVER HAVE THE LIFE YOU WANT, LET ALONE THE WORLD YOU WANT. At those times, you forget how far you have come, and instead focus only on how far you have yet to go.

Look around you. See the beauty, love, abundance, and opportunities that you have created. Yes, there is more to come (I guarantee it). But you've also come a long way. You've healed, you've grown, and you have created some wonderful realities.

So I have a suggestion: JUST FOR TODAY, AS OFTEN AS YOU CAN, ALLOW YOUR HEART TO FILL WITH GRATITUDE.

Instead of focusing on what is yet to come, or what is going wrong, spend this day focusing on what is here and what is going right. You and I both know that there is SO much to be grateful for right where you are—from the littlest things, like the beauty of this day, to the biggest things, like the fact that you are loved by those in your world and beyond.

As you feel this glorious energy of gratitude, I'll let you in on a little secret: One of the reasons my life is so amazingly fabulous is that I feel grateful every single day, many times a day!

And oh, past self, how my life has changed since starting that practice. There is more and more and even more to be thankful for, each and every day.

There is nothing I would change in my life. And, I promise: YOU WILL BE HERE SOON, IF YOU FLOW THE FEELINGS THAT WILL DRAW YOU HERE.

With loads of love and gratitude for you,

your future self

PS: No, I still won't tell you the winning lottery numbers—and you know why. You've won something better than the lottery: you create your own reality. Just wait until you get better at this. You will laugh with joy from morning til night!

82

FROM YOUR GUARDIAN ANGEL

the love continuum

You know, from our perspective (which is waaaay back), it appears as if your life
is one long continuum of love.

As we observe you on this continuum, we see that your world reflects your level of self-love.
On one end, you could have absolutely NO love for yourself, and on the other you could have
total, unconditional love for yourself.

THE MORE YOU LOVE YOURSELF, THE MORE WONDERFUL THINGS
YOU CREATE. You allow more love, more abundance, more joy, and more elegance and
ease in every regard. The more you love yourself, the more you allow the healing, and the
beautiful manifestations that reflect that love and healing.

Now, we can hear you, dear one, and you are thinking, "Well that sounds great, Angel, but
exactly HOW do I do that?"

First, FORGIVE YOURSELF FOR ALL THE CREATIONS IN YOUR LIFE THAT
WERE LESS THAN BEAUTIFUL. Forgive yourself for needing healing at all—
for change always begins with forgiveness.

Next, be gentle with yourself. Treat yourself as if you were a vulnerable, innocent, loving alien being, visiting this planet for the first time—because, in a way, that is what you are.

As you unload the armor of your past, you will begin to allow your true self to shine through.

I love you. More than you can know. Until we talk again, be gentle with you ...

your guardian angel

83

FROM YOUR SPIRIT

Feel The Burn!

I love you.

I don't just "love" you. I L-O-V-E you! I love you with passion, with commitment, and with overflowing joy!

Why do I make that distinction? Because I am the unseen friend who lights a fire in your belly and sparks a yearning in your soul.

And when you allow me to get close to you, that fire, that heat, creates!

You see, WHEN YOU LET YOURSELF FEEL YOUR PASSIONS, YOUR DESIRES, YOUR HOPES AND DREAMS DEEPLY, THEY WILL MANIFEST.

It is I, your spirit, who makes you feel alive! And it is that same energy—*my* energy, that excitement and expectation—that makes your dreams come alive.

So, here's an idea: WHY DON'T WE WORK TOGETHER? Why don't you let me help you make your dreams come true? Why don't you imagine me (gently) pointing out the beliefs that need changing in order to create those dreams?

TOGETHER, WE ARE A FORCE TO BE RECKONED WITH!

So dream your biggest dreams, feel the excitement and joy in knowing that *you* are the one who decides if they come true, and then commit to learning precisely how to make them happen.

In the meantime, don't forget to ask for my help. I have to obey those darned rules on your planet, and I can only do so much for you … until you ask!

With love and joy,

Your Spirit ♡•♥♡•

84

FROM THE GODDESS

Trust Yourself

I am grateful to have this way to talk to you, because I have a very important message for you.

I WOULD LIKE TO ASK YOU TO TRUST YOURSELF.

Please, trust yourself.

You see, my love, I feel you wondering about your decisions, about whether your dream will manifest, about who to trust, about whether or not you've chosen the "right" thing, and even about how you should be spending your time.

I see anxiety seeping into you, even as you seek to avoid it, and I see that anxiety (and your lack of trust) making your life less than the fun, free, exciting adventure it could be.

And so, I beseech you: slow down, enjoy life, and know that you are creating perfectly.

YOU CANNOT DO THIS WRONG. THIS IS NOT A TEST. Time will never run out, and the only measure of success is your own joy and happiness. Any other measure is not yours, but your ego's.

You see, if you let go of the comparisons and the doubt, what you are left with is *choice*. Ask yourself: "Does this feel good? If not, what does?" Once you know what feels good, you can choose again.

THIS LIFE OF YOURS IS A GIFT TO YOU. ALL YOU NEED TO DO IS ACCEPT IT, AND ENJOY IT.

With the deepest and most profound love imaginable,

The Goddess

85

Use Your Imagination

I'M EXCITED THAT YOU ARE HEADING INTO A NEW PHASE OF LIFE!

You do know, don't you, that everything can be different now?

I don't mean you could look at life differently. I mean LIFE CAN BE DIFFERENT.

How different? That depends. How much different can you imagine your life being? Because if you don't imagine your life different, it won't *become* different.

Yes, that is right: you can imagine your world exactly the same as it is now. The same challenges, the same difficulties, the same issues, the same worries. Or you can imagine unlimited abundance, "lucky" breaks, exciting opportunities, and even peace on Earth.

YOUR IMAGINATION IS THAT POWERFUL. Isn't that exciting?

However, there is one small detail that you should probably pay attention to. You can dream and imagine an amazing life for yourself, and even a wonderful new world to live in—but if you don't *believe* those wonderful things can happen, they won't.

However, you can change your beliefs. (And who would know that better than me, right?)

ONCE YOU CHANGE YOUR BELIEFS, THERE IS NO LIMIT
TO WHAT YOU CAN CREATE.

Now that IS exciting, eh?

With much love and support,

Your Subconscious Mind

PS: If you have forgotten precisely HOW to change those beliefs, no worries.
Just go to LiveALifeYouLove.com and learn the technique.

86

FROM THE CHRIST CONSCIOUSNESS

LOVE IS WHY YOU CAME HERE

So many on your planet focus on the differences between races, religions, and people. They want to make one type of being, human, talent, temperament, or point of view "better" than all the others.

They are missing the point. THE POINT IS LOVE.

LOVE IS WHY YOU CAME HERE.

Love is what you yearn to receive, and to give.

No matter the days you call sacred, the language you speak, or the traditions you hold dear, you have one gift more powerful than anything that ever was.

· LOVE.

I connect with you, here, today, in this moment, loving you so deeply, so unconditionally that, if you could let in even a tiny portion of that love, you would never, ever want for another thing as long as you lived.

For if you really felt the love I have for you, oh dearest one, you would automatically love yourself, and thus create a heaven for yourself on this very Earth.

So, my love, I pray, let it in.

LET IT IN.

And once you do, let it spill over onto everything, and everyone, with whom you come into contact.

With unending love,

THE CHRIST CONSCIOUSNESS

REMEMBER ...

IN THIS ILLUSION YOU CALL YOUR PHYSICAL WORLD,
SOME PERIODS OF LIFE ARE MORE CHALLENGING THAN OTHERS.

During these challenging times, you tend to forget you are a god-being. You tend to forget that I am here for you, ready to guide you to your highest joy. You tend to forget that you (always) create it all.

And, because there is so much to do, and so many (internal) demands to meet, you also tend to create more struggle and strife than you want or need to create.

However, sweet human self, it *can* be different.

YOU CAN CHOOSE THE WAY YOU WANT YOUR DAY TO GO AHEAD OF
TIME. AND THAT CHOICE WILL MAKE A DIFFERENCE.

Remember, you do not have to give up too much of yourself in order to love others. You can learn to love in a new way that is, first and foremost, self-loving. That beautiful self-love will spill over onto all those around you, and they will feel more loved by you than ever before.

Remember also to have compassion for those who are not as healed, as wise, or as aware as you are. You can help them, as well as yourself, by becoming a living example of self-love.

HERE IS AN INTENTION FOR YOU, SWEET ONE:

"I intend to enjoy my times with my coworkers, family, and friends to the highest degree I am capable. I intend to allow my interactions and communications to be easy, elegant, and surprisingly delightful. I intend to participate in only those projects and activities that bring me joy."

YOU ARE ABSOLUTELY, POSITIVELY, 100% IN CHARGE OF YOUR REALITY, ALL THE TIME. Let's make this a lifetime to remember, together!

With so much love for you,

YOUR HIGHER SELF

88

FROM YOUR SOUL

You Are Courageous

I want you to know something. This journey we are on together … It's epic.

You are blazing a trail that has never been traveled before. You are braver than brave. You are downright *courageous*.

And although you feel as if you are doing this alone, you are not. I AM WITH YOU EVERY STEP OF THE WAY. I know you can't see me (that is against the rules), and you can't hear me (also forbidden). But, my love, you can *feel* me.

If you are quiet, and you listen with your heart, you can hear my messages. You can feel my love, and you can benefit from my guidance.

THE MORE YOU PRACTICE LISTENING, THE BETTER YOU WILL HEAR.

At this stage of your journey, it is more important than ever to learn to quiet your mind and connect with me. For other than these messages you read in this book, I don't have a lot of options for connecting with you. I cannot call you on the phone, or text you on your cell.

I have to be subtle, and wait until you come to me.

I could help you so much more if you asked—and you would receive the answers so much better if you listened for them. Together, we could be quite a force.

JUST REMEMBER: YOU CREATE IT ALL, AND I AM HERE TO ASSIST.

Nothing is beyond your ability, especially when I help! Let's start right now.
Think of me, and I'll send a loving, empowering thought straight to your mind!

So, until we talk again, remember …

I love you eternally,

Your Soul

FROM THE AUTHOR

ACKNOWLEDGMENTS

Deepest appreciation and love to my husband, Richard—my favorite "seen friend"—for your support, love, and unending belief in me. And to my sons, friends, and family, thank you for being there, by my side, day in and day out, as we create this exciting experience on planet Earth together.

To my readers of the weekly Messages From Your Unseen Friends e-mails: this book was made possible by you. It's your comments, love, sharing, and feedback that prompted me to publish these words in book form. And thanks especially to D'Anne Barrett, who wrote the e-mail that pushed me over the edge.

To my editor and graphic designer, Bryna René Haynes: I consider myself one lucky woman to have the honor of working with you (even though I know I created you)! You are brilliant, creative, and a joy to collaborate with. Thank you, thank you, thank you.

And finally, to my unseen friends: I'll love you forever—or, as Lazaris (one of my most cherished unseen friends) would say, "forever and a day."

ABOUT THE AUTHOR

BONI LONNSBURRY

Boni Lonnsburry is an author, blogger, speaker, and expert in conscious creation.

Boni grew up in New York State, and started an MBA and a JD, completing all but a year of both degrees before realizing it wasn't her bliss. She then discovered the law of attraction, and it has been her passion ever since. At first, applying it was easier said than done, and she struggled mightily with finances, career direction, love, and success.

Her choice to put happiness first began her epic journey out of struggle. She began a company with a $50 investment and grew it to a $5 million company. In the process, she transformed her financial life from bankruptcy to abundance beyond her wildest dreams.

She then tackled her love life—which had been a challenge most of her life—and created the love of her life at the age when most people give up hope. She and her husband Richard were married in Fiji in 2010.

Boni wrote *The Map: To Our Responsive Universe, Where Dreams Really Do Come True!* so that others could follow a step-by-step process to create a life of their dreams.

The Map was an overnight success, winning seven book awards the first year, including the prestigious Nautilus Award and the "Best Law of Attraction Book" of 2013 by LOA Leaders.

Boni and her husband split their time between homes in The Bahamas and Boulder, Colorado.

Learn more about Boni and her work at LiveALifeYouLove.com.

Made in the USA
Middletown, DE
11 December 2015